SURVIVING THE
DEVIL

SURVIVING THE
DEVIL

AN ACCOUNT OF ADOPTION AND ABUSE

ANGIE COX

TATE PUBLISHING
AND ENTERPRISES, LLC

Published by Tate Publishing & Enterprises, LLC
127 E. Trade Center Terrace | Mustang, Oklahoma 73064 USA
1.888.361.9473 | www.tatepublishing.com

Tate Publishing is committed to excellence in the publishing industry. The company reflects the philosophy established by the founders, based on Psalm 68:11,
"The Lord gave the word and great was the company of those who published it."

Book design copyright © 2014 by Tate Publishing, LLC. All rights reserved.
Cover design by Allen Jomoc
Interior design by Jimmy Sevilleno

Published in the United States of America

ISBN: 978-1-63063-945-7
1. Biography & Autobiography / Personal Memoirs
2. Family & Relationships / Abuse / Child Abuse
14.02.11

DEDICATION

To all the victims of abuse—we are survivors.

CONTENTS

INTRODUCTION

MY TWIN DAVID and I did not have what you would call a "bed of roses" childhood. We endured the worst kind of physical, sexual, and emotional abuse. It wasn't until my adult years I realized how my childhood sufferings were relevant to kids I had volunteered to help in a neighborhood. My eyes were opened; there were countless children who were in a similar situation as I was.

Angie, I told myself, *you could really turn a negative into a positive.* From there, I realized I needed to write my haunting experiences down to open my world up. Suddenly I was a freight train. I had to get my story out. Even with life's hurdles and experiences, I kept telling myself I had to get the book out there. Why should I be ashamed to confront my past and reveal it to the world? I didn't do anything wrong. It took a long time to come to that point—that was progress in itself.

Too often, people tell abuse victims to just "get over it." I used to avoid bringing up my childhood at all costs, but people pushed and pushed. "Whatever happened with your family?" they wondered aloud. Then once it was out, it would inevitably come up. My childhood is often used against me. They'd say I act the way I do "because of my childhood," and I could "crack" at any moment. Initially I was sensitive about it, but I've finally gained a backbone and can hold my own.

That's why I'm doing this book. I want people to see that people are abused through no fault of their own. A life of abuse can cause terrible pain to the person years and years after it is done. Hopefully readers can put their feet in my shoes and understand how damaging abuse truly is, but I also want abuse victims to know they are not alone. If you have also been abused, I want you to know that you don't have to behave a certain way. It shouldn't skew your sense of right and wrong. There's always a decision to follow in the abusers' footsteps or not. You can change your path and chart it to the destination you want.

There's another side to being abused: a heightened sense of perception of everyone around you. Sometimes it makes you paranoid. Even if the abuse ended, whether physical or emotional, there's never truly an end to it. Nobody understands that more than I do. But we do not have to let childhood destroy us. There's always a way to turn the negative into positive.

This is my attempt to prove it while also understanding that it's much easier said than done to just "get over it."

For the rest of you, please open your eyes to abuse. This is what really happens in countless homes across the globe. There are often visible signs that abuse is occurring behind closed doors; don't be afraid to speak up for those kids when you see them. In David's and my case, it is chilling to think that so many people could have said something about what was being done to us. *They could have said something but didn't!* That fact used to keep me awake endless nights with alternating hope and despair.

But even though people inevitably have let me down, as with anybody, there are good people in the world too. My brother is an amazing person, and I never would have survived without him. Throughout this story, you will hear how we survived the abuse of monsters through children's eyes, but also the strength of twins—our struggles, our compassion, and our complete devotion to save one another no matter what the end brought.

That realization—the understanding that there are good people in the world who choose to do good no matter what cards they are dealt—*that* is what helps me move forward. That is what we need to focus on. In spite of how much evil is in the world, there are still so many acts of kindness and such fine people out there. I've chosen to keep my eyes on them instead of succumbing to the darkness.

THE UN-BIRTHDAY PARTY

IT'S NOT OFTEN a child comes face-to-face with the devil, but my twin brother, David, and I lived with him. "He" was actually a "she," and her name was Mrs. Lawrence, our foster mother.

Mrs. Lawrence was a short and stout middle-aged woman who only packed on weight as she aged. She looked like an upright walrus with a wig of long, greasy brown hair. The smell of it sticks with me even today. While Mrs. Lawrence was talkative and social, always inviting people to pop into her house, she showed David and I no affection whatsoever. I can't remember ever receiving an act of love, not even a hug. My memories are scarred with shouts and an endless list of chores. David and I constantly lived in fear of our adoptive mother, and we held no affection toward her.

Mrs. Lawrence's husband, Mr. Lawrence, was her foil. A quiet man, he was bald on the top of his head while black hair tufted around his ears. He was slim and cared about his appearance much more than Mrs. Lawrence, always sporting trousers and a button-down shirt. While his wife sat glued to the television, he was the one person who helped the house run smoothly (aside from David and me), always walking the dogs and preparing dinner.

Over the years of living with evil, it has become difficult to recall the parts that weren't hell. While David and I loved Mr. Lawrence, as he showed us nothing but kindness, he still never intervened in his wife's cruelty toward us. Rather than dwell on that, we try to remember the good: he was an agent for the pools, the betting pool based on top-league football matches. He liked gambling and always went to the dogs in Bournemouth on a Saturday and brought back chips. He smoked Old Holborn tobacco and embassy filter. Whenever I smell tobacco today, I think about his tragic role in our story.

The Lawrence's had three biological children, Nigel, the eldest, and Amanda and Rebecca. They were treated as any normal children, but we would discover that they took after their mother.

Everything had begun in the early hours of June 13, 1974, at 2:10 a.m. David and I entered into this intimidatingly large world in Holloway prison addicted to heroin. Our mother was serving a sentence for drug-related charges along with our father, and she had to wean us off the drug. Thankfully she was released soon after and took us home. We have been told that our mother was not able to take care of us because in her mental state, she was overwhelmed with two newborns. Our birth parents quickly decided to give us up to foster care, and when we were five months old, the Lawrences became our new parents.

My first memory was our fifth birthday. David and I were standing in the backyard against a wooden fence, David holding a ball and I a skipping rope. Our godmother, Mrs. White, was a Sunday school teacher and friend of Mrs. Lawrence's—that is, before she knew how she treated us. Mrs. White had given us those gifts and was taking a photograph of us, which was such a rare occurrence for us.

"Stand closer together," she said, smiling and motioning to us. When we were close enough for the camera, she held out an index finger. "There. Perfect."

David and I glanced at each other. *So that's what it's like.*

The photograph was deceiving. At that point, we still had unquestioning trust that is characteristic of young children. On our fifth birthday, the sun was shining, and we couldn't imagine any storm clouds. We were in the spotlight; the day seemed to hold promise. I held my breath in nervous excitement as we walked toward our postwar-era house. It looked so idyllic from the outside with the apple tree to the front, full of apples bursting with juice. The house was two-story and green trimmed. Its peaceful façade hid the horrors within too well.

When we returned inside, there were countless guests at our house, children running around having fun, shrill screams of glee, and sweets spread out on the table, but David and I froze next to Mum. Her voice was large and obtrusive in my mind: "Stay by me at all times." Just as she told us. The sweet smell of jelly and trifle was on the air, and we felt as warm as the sausage rolls cooling on top of the stove. So much good food— would we be able to eat it that time?

Shortly after our photographs were taken, Mum bent down toward David and me. I could see my bewildered face in the reflection of her glasses. "Get upstairs to your room, now." The smell of the foods she had been cooking and sampling lingered on her breath. Even though she had been working hard all day for this party, we wouldn't experience it. We wouldn't dare defy her.

Next I knew, I sat on my bed listening to everyone laughing and having a joyful time. *Why can't I be downstairs? This is our day*, I thought glumly. What kept the tears at bay was the possibility that maybe, just maybe, someone would come upstairs to see us and invite us back downstairs. I looked down at the ruffled, flowery party dress. Why on earth was I wearing a dress and had my hair done prettily? Didn't anyone else find it strange that we weren't at our own birthday party? Maybe they'd ask where we were. Maybe somebody missed us.

Over the course of a couple hours, the voices downstairs became softer, less chaotic. I heard the door open and close as they slowly filtered from the house. Finally Mum's voice from the staircase: "Angela and David, get down here now!"

My heart started to race. I looked at David and he at me, and we held each other for a moment.

"It's gonna be okay," David whispered to me. He squeezed my hand.

I looked at his large blue eyes. They looked so uneasy. "Yeah, it will. I love you."

"Love you too."

Our hands clasped together another few moments, we started to summon the courage to go downstairs.

David led the way, and the door opened with a creak. Then slowly, we went downstairs. Mrs. Lawrence was standing there with her arms crossed and her upper lip curled. We suddenly felt looked down upon, disgusting.

"Go into the living room," she barked.

We didn't know what we would see there. I gulped. As we got closer though, I saw a mountain of gifts that people had bought for David and me. A flicker of hope at last, but we were cautious.

David and I were holding each others hands tightly when Mum turned to the pile of gifts and distributed them among her own children. She then pivoted on her heels and jutted her doughy face close to our faces, so close I could smell her breath. "This is how much I hate you both. These gifts were yours, and now they are theirs. You don't deserve anything because you are little bastards. That is why your mum didn't want you...

because she knew you were little bastards! She hated you as much as I hate you!"

After her maniacal rant, we stood there and watched as her children opened our gifts. The excitement on their faces should have been our excitement. Greedily they took every gift and ripped the shiny paper off. After each box was unwrapped, they made sure to throw a mean comment at us.

"That sweater would have looked good on you, Angie. Too bad!"

"Oh look, an action man! Oh well. Girls, just pretend that it's David. Tear off its legs."

I felt a hot teardrop slipping from my eye and hoped that no one would see it. Of course, Mum did.

"What are you crying for?" she asked. "Here, I'll give you something to cry about." She then punched me on the side of my head so hard that I fell to the floor, pulling David down with me because our hands were still gripped together. He didn't want to let go, so we both lay there on the floor, covering our heads as she began kicking us. Grabbing one of my pigtails, she pulled me through the living room and up the stairs.

"No!" I screamed. I felt like my hair was ripping out in her hands as she pulled me. My knees burned as the carpet tore at my skin. Finally at the top, she yanked my hair so hard it pulled me up to standing. She kicked me in the back so I dropped once again.

"Stand up!" she yelled after dragging me into the bedroom. Once I stumbled to my feet, she pushed me forcefully to where I fell to the floor again. My head bounced upon impact. I lay there for a few minutes, still as a statue, too frightened to move because I knew if I got up, she would kick me down until I had no more tears to cry and no more strength to get up.

Suddenly the door slammed. She was gone.

It took me a while to lift myself up to the bed. I dragged myself across the room to the mirror. Once in front of it, I looked and saw a little pale face with such sad eyes. My white-blonde hair was disheveled. I looked like a fallen angel.

What have I done to let God hurt me so badly? I wondered. The question hung over me so heavily that I immediately fell to my knees and squeezed my eyes shut.

"Dear God, I try to be good. Please tell me why you don't love me, or else why would you let her hurt me? I am sorry if I was bad. Please forgive me and make her stop. I love you, God. Amen."

I stared into that mirror until my eyes hurt, hoping to see a happy, bright face looking back at me so I would know I was just having a bad dream. But that happy face never looked back. All I saw were that day's bruises marring my white skin. Retreating to my fantasies, I found myself imagining Mum coming up the stairs into my bedroom, saying how sorry she was that she hurt me, and then she would give me love and hugs. Then I closed my eyes and went to my horse.

The sky was a placid blue and the field bright green. I moved aside the grasses, as tall as I was, and toddled over to a majestic chestnut horse munching away in a field. Once he saw me with his liquid black eyes, he gently bent down for me as I stroked his head. Soon I rested against his belly. I felt the sun beating down on me and heard the birds singing as I moved with the rise and fall of my horse's breathing. Finally I was at peace. I wanted that feeling to never end unless it was

peace. I wanted that feeling to never end unless it was to become reality.

But my twin interrupted my retreat. David came upstairs to the bedroom, rushed to me, and held me. He was wild-eyed and upset. "I'm sorry I couldn't hold on anymore. You okay?"

"Yes." I paused. "Why does she hate us?"

"I don't know," David replied softly. "Do you want to play our game?"

I nodded.

We both got into bed and started to play our secret game. We would hum a song and have to guess what it was. Or if we were separated, we would have to knock the song on the wall and guess. We had hours of fun playing "name that tune."

David went first. His face lit up in a grin when he decided, and he joyfully tapped out the rhythm. I smiled when I realized what it was and quietly sang along. "Happy birthday to you, happy birthday to you! Happy birthday, dear David-and-angie, happy birthday to you."

"Ha-ha, I liked how you fit both our names in the same beat."

"My turn!" I said.

David and I played the game for a while and then told each other happy birthday. Once we couldn't hear Mrs. Lawrence's heavy footsteps downstairs, we breathed easier. She must have been preparing for bed. Once she did, it was always much easier for us to go to bed. Otherwise my stomach turned with each moved she made, and I wouldn't sleep at all.

The next morning, we awoke to Mum's yells as usual, but it was unusually early. As we filed up downstairs, we eyeballed the house, still a mess from the party. Soiled dishes were carelessly thrown in the sink and sitting atop the counter. Wrapping paper littered the brown living room carpet.

"Clean it up," Mum said. Then after a yawn, she retreated to bed, the floorboards creaking under her. David and I knew we had to be very quiet while we were cleaning. The last thing we needed was to wake her. In spite of the fact that my body was aching from the beating I received last night, I piled the dishes and began scrubbing. I had to learn to pretend it didn't hurt because in just a few hours, I would go to school, and nobody could learn that I was in any pain. If they did, all hell would break loose.

As we picked up the wrapping paper from our gifts, my heart hurt, and I felt a lump in my throat. I was so angry like I never had been before. Tears stung my eye, and I slammed down the trash bag that we were stuffing with trash.

"Why did she do this to us?" I asked. My voice broke as I started to cry.

"Shh!" he said, his head darting left and right. "You'll wake her."

I knew I should stop, but I was crying so hard that I just couldn't. It was like removing the foundation from a wall, causing it to crumble down. The sobbing was inevitable. Either Mrs. Lawrence was worn out from the previous day or she heard and didn't care because we somehow managed to finish cleaning up. Once she left her room, she surveyed the house with her beady eyes. I held my breath as I waited for her response. "Get ready for school," she finally said.

Once we came downstairs, Mum inspected David and I before we left for school. She made sure we were as messy and stinky as possible. We were not to clean or brush our teeth and wore oversized hand-me-down clothes that had belonged to her children who were much larger than David and me. There was no question that she derived great pleasure in knowing that the other children would tease us at school. Truly, there was no way she wanted us to have friends or any kind of fun or happiness in our lives. This was strategic; it covered her tracks because the bruises on our bodies could be attributed to the bullies at school.

I don't think there was a day we went to school that we were not bullied. The kids hated me, calling me stinky and ugly, and they pushed me around. Kids walked up to the teachers and said they couldn't sit by me because of how badly I smelled—on more than one occasion.

David and I got to school on that day after the party. As soon as we sat down for class, all the kids were teasing and laughing at us. "Where were you at your own party?" one sneered. "You didn't even open your gifts!"

My ears reddened. Soon I heard the clacking of heels behind me and saw that our teacher hovered above us. "What's going on?" she demanded.

"Nothing," David mumbled, staring at his hands.

"They had a weird birthday party," one girl piped up. "They didn't even open any gifts."

"They just hid upstairs," another kid said.

The teacher's brow furrowed, but she asked no more questions. As her skirts swished by and she walked away, a seed of worry started sprouting inside me. What if the teacher told Mum later? She would think we were complaining or that we had told them the horrible things she had done to us the night before. I wondered and worried all day. If she found out, our lives would not be worth living. I shuddered at the thought. The torture of thinking about it was getting to be too much. David knew I was worried, which was making him more nervous.

Our walk home that day was long; we were trying to come up with a story just in case something had been said until we realized nothing would get us out of her evil clutches. We walked into the house with our hearts racing and our hands sweating. Upon entering, I shakily exhaled.

"Get to work," she said from her normal spot on the couch. David and I glanced at each other. Just the normal nastiness, thank God.

We quickly put our bags away and started our chores, hoping that she would leave us alone that day if it were possible. We always had a lot of chores to do. Mum did not go to work, but she didn't lift a finger around the house either. That's what David and I were for. The most she did was instruct us on what to do and beat us afterward regardless of how well we cleaned. For someone who wanted the house so clean, she sure was a messy person.

David and I cleaned before and after school and then again after dinner. Whether or not she would let us eat was always the question on our minds. She had a very particular way of doing chores, and if they were not done "correctly," we were in big trouble. There were no guidelines on how to do it correctly, and there would be no way that she would *ever* forget to check our work. It was what she waited for all day long. A huge smile cut her pudgy face in half as she found something wrong— she thrived on the sport of beating us. She would not stop until her voice box wouldn't work anymore and her spittle stopped flying. Our screams would not matter; she didn't care about us. She just cared about her next opportunity to use us as punching bags.

While I wiped down the tabletop, I glanced over at Mrs. Lawrence's children. They were also laying in the living room, but normally they watched David and me; it wasn't uncommon for them to throw objects at us, poke us in the back with their fingers, slap us in the head, and laugh at us.

Rebecca and Amanda walked over that day with smirks on their faces. "Who can hit 'em the hardest?" Amanda asked.

"I'll get 'im on the floor," Rebecca said. They both laughed as if it were the funniest joke in the world before they enacted their threats.

Accustomed to the pain, I learned to block it well. When they hit me, I would pray to God to take the pain. *God, I know somewhere in your heart you have love for David and me. Take our pain away. With every punch, let me feel your strong arms around me instead. Please. I know you love us.*

THE MYSTERIOUS POT

WHEN I WOKE up, I immediately knew something was different about the day. I was awake, but I didn't want to move—my sore muscles felt like they were melted into the sheets. I felt total relaxation. My eyes opened and were directed toward the window. It was still dark. When my head rotated to the tiny alarm clock in my room, it said it was 7:00 a.m. Normally it was light at that time. That could only mean one thing…

"David," I said excitedly, gently shaking him awake. "David! It's going to rain today!"

His eyes popped open and he slowly smiled. "Yeah?"

"Yes! Maybe it'll even storm." The black clouds outside looked angry, foreboding.

We both jumped out of bed and hurriedly got ready for the day, eagerly anticipating the pleasant pitter-patter of raindrops on the roof. Once that happened, we were guaranteed a few hours of peace. In the meantime, the distant rumble of thunder made me squeal with the utmost excitement. Rainy days were better than Christmas in our world.

"Let's go down and see how she is," I said. David agreed.

We bounded downstairs with confidence we didn't normally have. Sure enough, Mum was dragging. Her slippers shuffled on the carpet; even her face seemed to drag. The bags under her eyes drooped, and her mouth turned downward. When we came downstairs, she looked at us with empty eyes.

"Do your chores," she said. She didn't sound forceful; it even sounded optional. David and I looked at each other questioningly and shrugged. We would do it until the rain came. Taking our stations at the sink, we glanced at the tall pile of dishes and held out hope that it wouldn't be our job to scrub them.

It was as if God answered our prayer. At that very moment, we heard pouring rain fall from the heavens. My heart leapt. I turned to Mrs. Lawrence. As if on cue, she slinked away into her room and quietly closed the door.

David looked at me with uncontainable excitement as he cracked a grateful smile. "We're free today," he said.

We didn't even go to school that day. No one would make us because Mr. Lawrence was at work. Once the others were gone, David and I leapt across the living room and pumped our fists in the air. Rainy days were free days because they depressed Mrs. Lawrence. She slept all day and kept the door to her room shut. There she hid until the sun shone again. It got to the point we almost cried when the sun rose. We were pale, tow-headed children, so we looked the part of creatures of the night.

One day, Mum had put a big pot of boiling hot water in the middle of the kitchen floor. I don't know why she did, but it was a recipe for disaster, which led me to believe it was on purpose. As usual, Mum ordered the girls—this time, Rebecca—to be horrid and chase David around the house to try to hit him. To make matters worse, the dogs were also hot on David's heels.

"Stop it, Rebecca!" Nigel yelled, visibly annoyed at their noise. I stood behind him, crying, because I hated seeing David get hit. Looking up at Nigel for direction, I suddenly heard a high-pitched scream. I peeked past Nigel's legs and saw David had fallen arms first into the pot of boiling water—the disaster waiting to happen.

Everyone ran into the kitchen to see what had happened, and there he was, lying on the floor cradling his arm and shrieking. Everything happened so fast; someone put hand towels onto his arms, and they stuck to his skin. Mum rushed him into the hallway and sat him down on the stairs. I stood there looking at him sympathetically, wanting to take his pain away. His screams intensified with time, and I broke down weeping for him.

"I can't take him to the hospital—oh Lord, I can't take him to the hospital! I'll get in trouble!" Mom kept repeating. Then she turned to David. "Stop crying!"

"It's not his fault," Nigel snapped. Before he could say another word, Mom snatched the towels off David's arms…pulling the skin with it. I had never heard him scream louder. It pierced the air like a knife before he vomited from the pain. The smell turned my stomach; his flesh was red and sore. As I watched on helplessly, I realized I had never wanted to help David so much in my life.

When is Mum ever going to stop? When is there ever enough *pain?* I thought.

There was no comfort from Mum. He was simply an inconvenience to her the one time he needed love the most. Nigel was aghast at the sight of David's arm and repeated, "You need to take him to the hospital. If not, I will."

He knew his mother too well. He ran to a neighbor's house and requested a ride to the hospital. Thankfully he consented, so Nigel returned, scooped David up, and left. Upon their departure, the house was uneasily quiet. Echoes from the ordeal reverberated throughout the empty hallways. Sick with worry for David and scarred from the experience, I quietly sniffed and walked upstairs. All afternoon, I never heard a TV or any voices, just silence for the first time in that house.

Later I looked out the window and saw Mr. Lawrence arrive home from work. My heart skipped a beat. Whenever he returned, the torture was never as bad. I put my ear to the bedroom door to hear what was going on downstairs. The deafening silence broke and gave way to yelling. Then the front door slammed. Mr. Lawrence left again, and I imagined it was to the hospital.

I looked around the empty room feeling devastated. The whole experience drained me, and I fell face first onto my pillow. I couldn't wait until Nigel came home; I had to know how my twin was and if he was ever even going to come back. Later, when the headlights rolled up the driveway, I only saw Nigel and Mr. Lawrence exit. My face fell; undoubtedly David would have to stay at the hospital for a while.

Evidently Nigel and Mr. Lawrence had a good story for that incident because no one asked any questions. I guessed that they had told the hospital that David was playing too close to the stove and knocked the pot off. They made it out to be a complete accident, and of course, they must have been very convincing as a "good church-going family." What else could have happened? If they only knew!

During the next few days, I missed David and never felt so completely alone before. It was the Lawrences against me. I knew Mum hated me even though she was trying to be somewhat lovely toward me; I knew what was going on. The whole reason they were kind to me was so that if anyone pressed questions on me, I wouldn't say anything against them. It wouldn't have worked anyway because I was too frightened.

The one silver lining of the experience was that the next few days were as peaceful as could be even though I was worried sick about David. Mum didn't beat me, but I still had my chores. She even let me stay downstairs with them, which was very unusual. I didn't care. It gave my body a chance to heal. After school, I would come home, do a few chores, and eat dinner with them. She then let her own children do the dishes while I watched TV.

"Go on then, what are you waiting for?" she asked. She shooed me to the living room and even gave me the remote. I glanced up at the kids, who looked clueless in the kitchen. Undoubtedly it was their first time cleaning up after themselves.

That night I stayed up late and almost enjoyed their company. It was nice to see Mr. Lawrence more than anyone else. His gentle presence around me warmed my heart, though I couldn't help but feel sad for him. He was also in Mum's evil clutches; she was always mean to him even though he worked so hard for his family. I never remembered him raising his voice, let alone laying a hand on David and me. Mr. Lawrence knew I missed David, so when no one else was around, he would cuddle me and comfort me as he held me close. I remember the feeling of his sandpapery chin on my head as he told me he loved David and me very much.

"I'm so sorry about all the bad things that have happened to you," he murmured so Mum wouldn't hear. "I promise I'll try to stop it. I can't take seeing you two get hurt." He tried to explain to me that when you love someone and they are hurting, it hurts you too. "I don't like that hurt. I feel it in my heart all the time. Enough is enough."

I believed him and trusted that it would all go away, just like I had asked God so many times. Maybe Mr. Lawrence was an angel sent to deliver us. Pleased with that thought, I let my head fall against his shoulder and enjoyed the warm comfort I so infrequently enjoyed but so frequently craved.

When David finally came home, I was stunned because it was a happy occasion. All the attention was on him, which relieved me because the last thing he needed was any more harm. When he walked in, I saw his arms bandaged up, so I hugged him gently, even though all I wanted was to squeeze him because I had missed him so much.

While the rest of us were relieved, Mrs. Lawrence could only worry about one thing.

"What did the doctors ask? What did you tell them?" she asked her husband. She didn't care a bit how David was, even though she was trying to be more accommodating for whatever reason. As I saw her wringing her doughy hands in front of Mr. Lawrence, my dislike of her skyrocketed to new levels.

That night Mum made a party-style dinner complete with sandwiches, pork pies, sausage rolls, ice cream, and jelly. The room was bright with high spirits and smiles. All I thought was what Mr. Lawrence had said about stopping the bad things. His promise came true! I grinned and couldn't wait to tell David that things were going to be different now. Imagining him smiling back at me and feeling the happiness I felt was enough to make me get up and dance. We were finally a part of their family! I told myself it meant that they loved us. In celebration, I helped myself to one more overstuffed little pork pie.

The next day, our social worker Mr. Mole came around to see David. Whenever he visited, I always got nervous; could I finally tell him what Mum was doing to us? Usually she just sat there and rattled off all the "bad things" David and I had done. There were no questions of "How are you doing?" or "What's been going on at school?" Instead Mr. Mole looked at us seriously and lectured us about how wrong we were to give Mrs. Lawrence trouble.

"You should be thankful for them, you two. They have given you a loving home and a loving family," he said seriously.

Whenever he came over, it was the one time we were made to look nice and clean. *He should come to school and see how I look then*, I thought bitterly.

Prior to his visit, Mum scurried around breathlessly. As she buttoned my cardigan up, she said, "You know what to respond with when he asks about David. So stick to it."

As we expected, Mr. Mole did ask me, and I told him exactly what I was instructed. David followed suit. Mr. Mole's brow furrowed, and he frowned, but he seemed satisfied with the answers. He handed David a get-well gift and said good-bye. After the door closed behind him, Mum promptly snatched the gift from David. "You can open it after dinner," she said stiffly. From there, she led us into the kitchen to set the table.

All throughout dinner, David's eyes were glued to the gift wrapped neatly on top of the counter. After it was over, he timidly asked he if could open the gift.

"You're a greedy bastard," Mum said. "Aren't you happy enough to have your arms? You should think yourself lucky! Nigel was stupid enough to take you to the hospital. I would've let you suffer. Now get to bed."

My eyes locked in with David's. He was crestfallen. With Mr. Mole's departure and Mom's refusal to let him have the gift, I knew things were bad again, and that was never going to change.

❧⳥⳺

Although I spent the night mourning the loss of the future we thought we had, strangely the next day, David was allowed to lie down on the sofa. I glanced at her uneasily. She had a smile on her face, but it looked odd, like she was a Mr. Potato Head with angry eyes and the wrong mouth. We never knew about Mum because her moods shifted like the wind, but at least for the next few days she was nice again.

"Be nice to David," she warned her kids. It was too tall an order for herself, let alone her kids.

Sickness Is No Solace

One morning, I woke up feeling warmer than usual and extremely itchy. I looked down at my arms and saw they were covered in red spots. To my right, David was still asleep but pale and covered in the same spots. Even though I knew it was fruitless, I hoisted myself out of bed and crept to Mum's room. Maybe she'd be less hard on us while we were ill.

Once I saw her mountainous shape under the covers, I whispered, "I'm not feeling well."

She turned over. "Go back to bed."

That was all I needed to send me hurriedly walking from bedroom. Once I returned to David, I saw him in fetal position. His spotted face grimaced. I climbed back into bed and hoped against all odds that we'd be given a free pass that day.

When our bedroom door opened, Mum walked in. "Get up and go downstairs."

I summoned all my strength and tried to tell myself I'd be okay, that chores wouldn't be that bad. However, David distracted me; he wasn't getting out of bed. Silently I prayed that Mum would be merciful. To my shock she must have been in a good mood for a little bit because she scooped David up and carried him downstairs!

Once she set David down on the sofa, she felt our foreheads and looked our bodies up and down. "You're fine," she said simply. "Now go get your chores done."

I knew that we were not fine: my whole body was itchy, and I was overheated and fatigued. My daydreams turned to thoughts of lying down. That's all I wanted. Mrs. Lawrence's dilemma, I realized, was that she could not take us to see a doctor because of all of the bruises. In turn we had to suffer; God, help us if something *really* went wrong.

Looking at David feeling so sick, I worked really hard to get the chores done for his sake. Afterward, it would inevitably be time for our potties.

Potty time had been going on for a long time. It wasn't that we had a problem with wetting ourselves; it was just another form of torture. David and I had to take all our clothes off and sit in the corner of the kitchen on the potties for hours until Mum said that we could get up, and unfortunately there was never a timeline for us sitting there. It was wholly up to Mum's whims. Our bums would get pins and needles and become numb, so I would try to focus on one area of the wall and just stare at that area until long blocks of time went by. I became really good at going off into my own little world, imagining that I was somewhere else living a different life. I used to imagine a field full of flowers, and I would roll around in the grass picking the flowers and running with David. There was nothing I enjoyed more than feeling the daydream's sun shining and hearing the imaginary birds singing.

That day we felt sick, both David and I were sitting on our training potties in the kitchen. Mine was white and David's was yellow. Sometimes we were put in the hallway, sometimes we were separated, but the aspect that remained the same was that we were both completely naked for hours at a time. That day he was right beside me. Mum used to make us sit on the potty every morning, and we would sit there until she decided we had been sat there for long enough. This went on until we were approximately eight years old, although in the latter years, it was not as often as every morning; it was only when she felt like humiliating us.

That day we were at the far end of the kitchen. David sat with the back door to his right-hand side, and I was sitting to his left with the stove to my left-hand side. On this particular occasion, I remember being forced to sit on the potty for a long period of time. The music on the credits of Mrs. Lawrence's shows marked each hour. Initially the seat was cold, and I saw goose bumps all over my body. Soon the tops of my legs and my bum had begun to go numb. My back was hurting, and I felt scared, although I always felt scared, so it was nothing new.

Once Mum finally walked into the kitchen, my lower stomach tingled nervously. *What is she going to do?* I wondered. First she walked over to David, grabbed him by his arm, and roughly yanked him up. She then roughly pushed him back onto the floor, where he fell on all fours. I didn't dare say a word or reveal my fear, but as she then put her hand onto the back of David's head and began to push his head into the potty, desperation ballooned in my chest. I *so* wanted to help him.

"Look at you! You're disgusting. You pooped in there, you disgusting thing!"

David was crying, and I was shaking knowing that she would do the same to me. He had a little pageboy hairstyle at the time, so there was enough hair for Mum to grab hold of and yank back his head. My eyes darted to him. Relief, there was no poo on his face.

"Here you are." Mum put her hand into the potty— I spoke too soon. After lifting up a messy handful, she started smearing it all over David's face. It really looked like she was trying to squash it into his mouth. David began to make these terrible gagging noises like he was choking. Mum's face was bright red from the struggle.

There was no one else in the room at the time; Dad was at work, and the other children were all at school. I could only watch in horror, feeling sick and helpless as David bawled.

"Now go upstairs and wash your face," she finally commanded. David immediately fled from the room in tears.

My turn.

Mum shouted at me to get up. She then slapped me on the head, saying, "Your mother knew you were going to be bastards. That's why she didn't want you. She hated you."

During the whole time she demeaned me, she hit me on the head about five times, and they weren't gentle slaps. As she moved close to my face, I could hear her grinding and gnashing her teeth—her habit whenever she was angry.

"Go empty your potty and go upstairs."

One small silver lining of the ordeal; I didn't want my own feces smeared on my face. Without looking at her, I grabbed my potty and ran outside.

The next day Mum realized that we had chicken pox. As a result, we were not to go to school and were forced to sit in the kitchen on our potties again. We were still naked and in the same formation, but this time we were covered in calamine lotion. Even though we were at home sick that day, I knew that the situation only gave

Mum more opportunity to do unnamable, horrid acts to us.

Sure enough, Mum walked over and grabbed ahold of my hair. I knew then that something bad was going to happen to me. As she pulled me by the hair, my potty tipped over.

"Now look what you've done!" Mum yelled, her face plum with anger. My eyes widened. I was in for hell.

"I'll show you! I'll show you!"

At that point I was back on my feet. Mum let go of my hair, dived for the kitchen drawer and grabbed a tablespoon. She waddled back to where I stood and scooped the contents of the potty and pushed it against my mouth. Wild-eyed I tried pursing my lips together as hard as I could, scrunching my mouth up so not one smear could enter my mouth. It wasn't enough. Mum was even stronger in her madness, and the spoon made it past my mouth. I then felt the spoon against my teeth, scraping against my gums.

"Open your mouth! Eat it! Open your mouth right now!" Mum was screaming and shouting; flecks of spit flew from her mouth and splattered on my face. I squeezed my eyes together as tightly as possible, tasting the iron from the spoon she pushed so roughly into my mouth. She had scraped my lower lip, now bleeding and also entering my mouth. Thankfully the majority of the poop had fallen off the spoon whilst she trying to force it in.

The mixture of blood, iron, spit, and the rancid smell of the poop got to me. I started heaving.

"If you get sick, I'm making you eat it!" she growled. I'll never forget how that day she wore a long-sleeved, shiny jade-green dress with big pastel flowers on it. While trying to collect myself, I stared at the ugly flowers and concentrated on keeping bile down. My eyes were watering, but I looked over at David sobbing in the corner so hard that he couldn't catch his breath.

After an eternity, Mum yanked me out of the kitchen and pulled me upstairs by my arm. She dragged me along the carpet as she usually did, but I was still naked and getting burnt by the rough upholstery on my chicken pox. Once upstairs, she threw me in the bathroom. She pushed me at an angle in order to get to the tap because nothing was ever done gently. Steam was coming from the tap and I could feel it on my face. Mum started to splash my face with the hot water. Before I could scream she turned the tap off and pulled me away from the sink by grabbing my hair. It hurt so much that I thought I was going to be sick.

There was no pattern to when things would happen to David or me when we were sitting on the potty. We constantly lived in fear. The routine was basically the same but with a few adjustments to make it scarier for us. Sometimes Mum would pour the contents of the potty over me and then wouldn't let me take a bath.

That night after Mum tried to spoon-feed me with poop, I laid in bed and prayed God would allow the illness to worsen so I could die and go to heaven. "Give me my wish," I begged. My whole body hurt, but my insides hurt more. I wasn't sure whether it was from what I had eaten or from the heartache.

As I lay in bed pondering, I wondered what our real mum was doing. Did she love us? Would she have treated us the same? Mum had never made it a secret that David and I were not her real children; she said that we were too ugly and stupid to be hers. We were "little bastards," and she would never let us forget it.

I absentmindedly stared at the mirror on the opposite wall. If I could just stop thinking about everything, it would be better for me. Then maybe I'd have some sort of resolve to keep myself from dying, from leaving David alone without an ally in the world.

That's when I spotted something. I shot out of bed and squinted closer at the mirror. The image made my jaw drop. There, behind me, was the silhouette of a man. The details are fuzzy because his eyes entranced me. They were gentle, and they twinkled at me. Then he smiled. When I blinked again, he was gone.

No! Come back! I mentally cried. I earnestly stared at the mirror in hopes he would return. At the same time I felt comforted with the knowledge he was watching me. I didn't need to think about it too hard. Every fiber of my being told me it was Jesus, without gaining any formal education on who Jesus is. For me, it was innate.

He never came back in that way, but he lingered in my memory.

⁂

The next few days were spent in our bedroom. Our light bulbs were taken out and we were given a bucket with which to relieve ourselves. Our food was limited to whatever Mr. Lawrence could give us. He was our godsend as he tried very hard to give us food and water, but he never put it on a plate to avoid having any evidence of his assistance. Sometimes, when he would go to the shops and get his paper and tobacco, he would bring us back sweets. First he would remove the wrappers and then he'd slip them under the door. Those treats are what sustained us in that tough time.

"What if we ran away?" I asked David.

"Where would we go?" he replied miserably.

We were so scared to tell anyone about what was going on. What if they didn't believe us? Would we still have to live with Mrs. Lawrence? Surely she would find out about our snitching, and then God only knew what hell awaited us.

The next day, I realized why Mum had not beaten us for a few days; we were to have a visit from Mr. Mole. During the whole visit, I was thinking about what would happen when he left. There was no doubt in my mind that Mrs. Lawrence would beat us to compensate for the last few days. My whole body started to shake with fear and the lingering sickness.

That's when I caught Mr. Mole's attention. He looked at me closely. "How long have these kids had the chicken pox? Have they seen a doctor?"

"Of course they have," Mum lied. He believed her— no surprise there. She was charming when she chose to be.

"Are you all right, Angie? You look very pale," he said.

"Yes, sir," I replied. I could feel Mum's eyes boring into me after his question. Mum had palpably evil looks. We always knew when she wasn't happy, and she was not happy right then.

What'll I do? This will be so bad. I gulped when I thought about what awaited me pending Mr. Mole's departure.

Once he left, the inevitable happened. Mum grabbed me and dragged me outside through the back door. "You think you have it tough? I'll show you," she whispered venomously.

She opened up the coal shed, threw me in there, and locked the door. It was dark and dirty, halfway filled with coal left over from the winter. Coal pebbles pressed into my back and chilled me to the bone.

"Let me out!" I screamed. Crawling through the coal, I made my way to the door and banged on it as hard as I could. At that young age, I was terrified of the dark. My whole body trembled, and I felt weak, but I continued to scream myself hoarse. However my screams only managed to bring Mum outside with a bucket full of water. She splashed it all over me and told me to shut up.

"Please let me out," I begged as she kicked the door in annoyance.

"The boogeyman is going to hear you if you don't shut up!"

I was crying so hard I couldn't catch my breath, and it didn't help that I was violently shivering from the cold water. To pass the time, I tried everything I could to get that door open, but it was no good. With that realization, I knew Mum had bolted it. There was nowhere to sit apart from atop the coal, and the sharp edges dug into my skin. There was no light, but I tried my best to move around until I could get somewhat comfortable.

Hours passed. I was starving and getting colder. I strained my eyes to try and see through the keyhole, hoping that David could get out. As I listened for any sound coming from the house, my eyes were stinging from my tears. I couldn't breathe from the coal dust. I sat on my hands to try and keep them warm before curling up in a ball and trying to sleep if at all possible, but the pain of the coal digging into my body was too much. Throughout the night, I heard noises that frightened me, probably the animals outside that I was unaccustomed to. Mum's boogeyman comment stuck with me the entire time.

Finally, hours later, the door opened. It was Mr. Lawrence looking at me sadly.

"Come inside and have some breakfast," he said softly. He awkwardly put his arm around me and led me inside, where he had made me eggs with toast and a warm cup of tea. David sat across the table from me, and as soon as I sat down, he grabbed my hand. I tried to squeeze his hand back, but I was so cold that my joints were stiff. I knew I had spent the whole night out there because my body was so cold and stiff that it hurt.

"Eat quickly, " Mr. Lawrence said, looking toward the doorway. "You know they will take that away from you if they come down here, so eat up." That wasn't a problem; we were half-crazed with starvation. It didn't help that it was the weekend, and we had no idea whether we would eat again that day or in a few days.

But Mrs. Lawrence was too quick for us to scarf down our food.

"What's she doing in here? Who let her out?" she asked, outraged.

"I did," Mr. Lawrence said. He straightened up so he could stand just a bit taller than his 5'8" height. "You left her in there all night! Are you trying to kill her?"

"That's a good idea. Less trouble for me."

"When did you become such a monster? They are children! They cannot fight back. When is it going to end?"

"The trouble is that you are a pushover!"

"No, you treat the animals better than you treat the twins. Why keep them just to treat them like this?"

Mr. Lawrence and Mum started to argue loudly, so David and I were sent out into the backyard, where we spent the whole day. We slumped down into the grass and picked at it, wondering the result of the fight.

"Maybe Mr. Lawrence will leave and take us with him," David said. "What a nice life we'd have then!"

"No one to beat us," I said slowly. "Maybe even love." We hoped and prayed for that day and wondered if it would ever happen. Though we were left alone outside for the majority of the day, we were at peace with our fantasies. That's all we cared about.

THE LONGEST SUMMER

RIGHT BEFORE SCHOOL ended, I found a friend: Sarah Davidson.

When we lived in the first house at 38 Mount Road, there was a family who lived all the way down the hill on the corner. When I walked down to the bottom of the hill, I could look straight ahead and see the house. That's where the Davidsons were—a couple with kind eyes and a den of cubs. Though they would do anything for anyone, Mrs. Lawrence sneered at them.

"Never seen a dirtier house!" she mumbled to me. "They smell awful, just like you and David!"

The daughter, Sarah, was my age and in my class. Because her family was poor and she wasn't well kempt, the other students picked on her. We exchanged know-ing looks whenever the taunting came.

I know. I've been there. Her eyes communicated to me. I extended the same courtesy.

We were each other's outlets, and we got along well. When we came back from lunch, we'd hear the jeers of students behind us: "Hey, piggies!"

My heart fell. Sarah would grab my hand and say, "C'mon." From there, we would run away together and try to find a place to hide. We often found ourselves in random janitorial closets and bathroom stalls, where we stood on the toilets so no one could recognize us by our ratty shoes.

On occasions, Mrs. Lawrence would let David and I go down to the Davidsons's house, not because she wanted to give us some fun, but because David and I had concocted a plan.

"I don't wanna go!" David cried. "They smell so bad!"

"It's miserable," I added.

"Please don't make us go!"

"Shut up!" Mrs. Lawrence would cut in. "You'll go over there because I say so."

David and I could barely contain our sighs of relief. Our little plan worked! We were able to go down there to play and have a great time.

Whenever we walked in, Sarah's mum greeted us meekly. "Hullo there," she said. She would open the door with a smile and gesture for us to come in. "Can I get you two something to drink?"

As soon as we walked in, the musty smell hit our noses, but I didn't care. I didn't see the piles of laundry and toys and dirty plates. All I saw was the rare sight of sweet, smiling faces. I drank it in.

"D-do you have any Coca-Cola?" David asked shyly.

"Of course, dearie," Mrs. Davidson said. "Any crisps too?"

We nodded fervently. Certainly the Davidsons could tell we were unusually thin; it was almost always the first thing people said about us. It was uncomfortable because we couldn't be truthful about how hungry we really were.

From there we walked upstairs to see Sarah. The stair carpet was soiled with cat fur and unnamable stains, and the banister had a few chips in it. We turned to the left and saw the yellow light dancing on the floor, coming from the television. It beckoned us inside Sarah's room, where we joyfully greeted one another and reveled in our rare opportunity for companionship with other human beings our own age.

While we watched movies upstairs with Sarah, Mrs. Davidson walked upstairs and presented before us a bountiful feast: crisps, Coca-Cola, and even candy!

"Thank you so much," David said. I was too happy to even speak.

"I'll make some sausage rolls later if you'd like," Mrs. Davidson said. At the mere mention, we began salivating. We nodded our heads so quickly our heads must have been a blur. Perhaps she was being so kind because Sarah needed a friend too. It was a match made in heaven.

There was no shortage of tragic days for either of us, but David experienced something no child should ever endure.

Eventually Nigel and David came to share a room when we grew older. Nigel was eighteen and David was eight. David was settled into bed and ready to sleep, but then Nigel came in. He saw Nigel's dark silhouette in the doorway before he turned the light on and illuminated the Elvis poster on the wall. Before David could adjust to the light, Nigel pulled his trousers down.

"Come down," Nigel said. David was on the top bunk so had to climb down to follow Nigel's order. He didn't want to defy Nigel; he was nicer to him than Mrs. Lawrence (even if that wasn't saying much).

Nigel told David him to open his mouth and suck his penis. He held David's head as he penetrated his mouth backward and forward. David did not know what to do; he just did what he was told. Though it lasted a couple minutes, it felt like hours. Then, all of a sudden, Nigel just stopped. Maybe he knew it was wrong. In any case it was never mentioned again.

Nigel never sexually abused him again, but that didn't mean he wouldn't make David's life hellish. Whether it was guilt or shame, Nigel's abuse of David triggered many beatings from that day forward. He wouldn't allow David to be in the same room as him, and he pushed him around at every chance he could snatch.

Thankfully it was short-lived: soon after this incident, Nigel joined the army.

However, I would discover years later that the other siblings proved to be another threat. Amanda was well into her teens, but strangely, she frequently called David into her room to discuss her girly magazines.

One night, while David was watching *Magnum, P. I.* on television, she had just come out of the shower. She stuck her head out of the downstairs bedroom and curled her finger in a "come here" motion toward David.

"I have something to tell you," she said, her head poking out of the doorframe.

David was confused, but he got up in spite of his concerns and entered Amanda's room. She closed the door behind him and said, "If you touch the towel I'm wearing, it'll come off."

Unwilling to do that, David tried dodging her and exiting the room at once. Amanda was too quick for him, though: she blocked the door, dropped her towel, and stood there naked. The next thing David knew, he was forced on the bed against his will, fully dressed underneath Amanda's naked body as she rubbed back and forth against him.

"The magazine says it's good for me," she explained briefly.

Eyes glued to the doorway, David whimpered. "I don't like it."

Mercifully she stopped and slumped back on the bed. "This is our secret," she said. "You are not to say anything. The magazine said it's good for you anyway."

David left the room.

For weeks, David was much quieter around everyone than usual. He spoke to me, but I noticed he seemed frightened, on edge. It didn't escape Mrs. Lawrence's attention, so she asked him what his issue was one night.

David told her. She said that he was lying and sent him out of the room.

Shortly thereafter, school was out for summer vacation, so we were outside in the backyard from sunrise till sunset, and Mum would never let us go anywhere. Sometimes they would go to the local swimming pool, but David and I were not allowed to play in the water unless Rebecca went into the water.

"When you get there," Mom began, speaking from her position at the steering wheel, "Rebecca, I want you to hold them down. Dunk them in the water."

David was a natural swimmer whereas I was terribly scared of the water. All I could think about was Rebecca holding me under; I would panic so badly that my body stiffened up and my lungs constricted, giving me even less oxygen. Right when I thought I was about to die because I couldn't breathe, Rebecca would release me, and I'd shoot up like a rocket, gasping for air. The traumatizing experience never failed to make me burst into tears every time, which Mum hated because we were in public. She'd grit her teeth together as she attempted speaking in a lower voice.

"Sit down and shut up," she'd say, "or I'll give you something to *really* cry about." Without a doubt, that was her favorite saying to me.

Other than these little outings to the pool, David and I were stuck outside in the backyard from morning until nightfall, and if not that, we were locked in our bedrooms. We had no toys to play with and no friends to come around, so it was just David and me. Even when we were put to work, I welcomed it because it made the bleak days go by faster.

Next door, there was an old man called Mr. Edwards, who Mum used as another weapon of fear against us. She put her face framed by her smelly hair right in front of ours and spoke through her teeth. "You know what Mr. Edwards does over there? Whenever he leaves his house, he kidnaps children so he can torture 'em. You know how he does that?"

I would shake my head ever so slightly just to appease her.

"Let me tell you. He cuts off children's fingers and toes off one by one. Don't get near him, or he'll take yours off too!"

Today I'd wager Mr. Edwards was a frightening-looking man not only for children but for adults too. He mumbled and didn't enunciate his words well so it sounded like he was speaking in tongues. Whenever Mrs. Lawrence went inside, he would stand in front of us and drop his pants. David and I were always on guard when we were outside for that reason, which is why she knew we were terrified and capitalized on that by making us sleep outside sometimes. Each night dripped by whenever we were forced to sleep outside with the dogs. My head would stay tilted to the left just to make sure he never ventured over to our yard.

Sometimes we would have a tent up, which we didn't mind because David and I were secluded and felt hidden. Despite being extremely scared of Mr. Edwards, we experienced a special closeness at night when everyone was in bed. We would not have to fear Mum pulling us out of bed and beating us because she knew that the neighbors would hear us if she came outside. Instead we could let loose, relax, and snuggle next to each other. It was very rare that we ever had affection, and when we did, it was only from each other.

Early in the morning, we would hear the sounds of other children playing, and it was like a sword to my heart. The screams of playfulness, the laughter, the happy sounds—all the jubilance of a normal childhood teased my ears and my mind. I cannot count how many times I closed my eyes and asked myself why David and I had the life that we had. Each long, sweltering day, I sustained myself with daydreams of finding my real mum and dad and having a fairy tale life, where I might have an actual majestic horse. I wanted David and I to be like the kids from school who could play on swings and to learn how to ride a bike.

Instead, that summer, Mum decided she wanted to plant a bunch of vegetables and flowers in the backyard, and of course, she wanted David and me to do most of the work.

Just another reason for her to yell at us, I thought uneasily.

I was right. For someone who never worked, Mum seemed to think she was the expert on how we should do each and every task.

"This isn't right!" She stomped. "You're not doing it right. Get over here."

She took me to the back door, opened it, and told me to put my fingers in the crack of the door where the hinges were. I turned and looked at her with eyes the size of saucers; I had no idea what this would lead to, but it wouldn't be good. As soon as I hesitantly put my finger on the hinges, she slammed the door, and my fingers got crushed. The throbbing was so painful I wanted to throw up, but all I could do was scream.

That's when our next-door neighbor on the other side came to the fence and yelled, "Is everything okay?"

Mum went round to see her and put on the most charismatic mask she could muster. "Ah, the little darling had just fallen. She's a bit of a drama queen, ya see."

Through the day, as I continued working with David, the lady was in her backyard and kept glancing at us. Once I was close enough, she asked me if I was all right. She glanced down at me cradling my hand.

"Can I look at it?" she asked gently.

My throat tightened. I wanted for this lady to help me, but the risk was too great. "I can't," I whispered. "She might see me."

Her eyes narrowed. "*Did* you fall this morning?"

I quickly replied no.

She winked at me. "Everything is going to be okay," she said. Then she rotated on her heels and quickly walked back to the other side of the yard. David was standing a few feet behind me, so he came walking forward when she was out of earshot.

"Did you tell her?" he asked.

I told him what she had asked and he replied, "Maybe she will help us!"

As if on cue, Mum came outside and leered at us. Grabbing my shoulder, she whispered, "If I find out you said anything, you will be real sorry."

I felt sick to my stomach.

For the next few days, I kept nervously glancing over my shoulder and wondering if anything became of the neighbor's questions. I was split into two. I wanted the neighbor to bring us help while also hoping *against* it in case Mrs. Lawrence gave me a beating for speaking up. Only time would tell.

I sat thinking about it as I swept the floor in the kitchen. Maybe a policeman would burst through the door and take away Mrs. Lawrence in handcuffs, and David and I could just live with Mr. Lawrence.

"Boom, boom!"

I blinked. My imaginings sounded real. I could actually hear someone at the door. Thing is, Mrs. Lawrence could too.

"Put that away!" she hissed. I did as I was told and put the broomstick against the refrigerator and walked into another room. When I heard the door opening, I couldn't help but turn around and glance at the visitor. It was a tall man I had never met before. He was unsmiling.

"Go!" Mrs. Lawrence mouthed. With that, I scurried away and could only hear indistinct, low muttering behind me. I would only have to hide for a couple minutes.

"Angie!" Mrs. Lawrence called out—not unkindly for once. "Come back over. This nice man wants to speak with you."

I came through the doorway from the other room and waited. The man eyed Mrs. Lawrence until she walked away to the direction of her bedroom. Only when we heard the door close did the man acknowledge me.

"Hullo there," he said softly. He put his hands on my shoulders and looked at me with eyes that seemed to bore into my soul. Something told me I wasn't in trouble. "Angela, I heard your hand got hurt. Can you tell me what happened?"

My eyes flit over to Mrs. Lawrence's bedroom door. The man saw my eyes go there, and the lines around his mouth deepened. "You can tell me. Don't worry about her," he assured me.

I didn't know who that man was or why he was there, but in seconds, I knew that telling him what actually happened would only help me. "Okay," I whispered. "She did it. She slammed my hand in the door."

He nodded gravely. "Would you be comfortable telling me if she did anything else?"

In spite of my earlier fears, I did tell him other details of abuse. I remembered how uneasy Mrs. Lawrence looked when he appeared at the door and realized I had nothing to be afraid of.

"Thank you for telling me," he said. He stood up and straightened out his back.

After he left, Mrs. Lawrence didn't do anything to me. Her eyes looked vacant when she exited the room. She looked through me instead of at me. Very queer indeed, but I firmly grasped at any shred of hope that this would end well for me.

Our social worker, Mr. Mole, also questioned us a couple days later. Mrs. Lawrence was again requested to leave the room at once. David and I sat stiffly in the best clothes we had, feeling ironically uncomfortable in well-fitting clothes and vulnerable in our cleanliness.

"Angela," he said, turning to me. "How do you feel living here? In general?"

My throat cracked when I started to speak, but I knew I could say what I needed to. After all, I never got in trouble for being honest with the other investigator. "W-well, honestly, I sometimes feel like… like Cinderella."

He nodded slowly. "Why's that?"

I explained that only David or I cleaned. I also said I didn't feel loved. His comments in the social services records indicate that he felt that there was some substance to this.

Interestingly enough, when Mr. Mole spoke to her later, she admitted that she hit me. "I intended to smack her legs, but I missed and accidentally punched her in the eye."

As ludicrous as the excuse was, social services never did anything further.

During that summer, we were sometimes sent to one place or another to be punished, usually by Mum's friends. There was never a true reason; she fed them lies so we would experience multiple sessions of discipline. Some of her friends would punish us, and some would just tell her that they had punished us when they really had not.

But there was one friend of hers that was cut from the same cloth. They would not allow us to be in their house. On the few occasions that they did allow us in their house, they made us sit in their closet under the stairs until we had to go home. Most of the time that we were there, David and I were not even allowed in the backyard, so we had to stand in the side alley so that the neighbors wouldn't see that we were out there for such long, hot hours—for up to eight to ten hours at a time with no food or water. Like Mum, this family liked to physically assault David and me, beating us with a belt, tree sticks, dog leashes, and anything they could find that would leave a mark and make us scream.

If David and I were not in the backyard or Mum's friends' houses during the summer holiday, we were locked in our bedroom. That was one of Mum's favorite punishments for us. When I was about eight years old, she locked David in his bedroom by tying rope to the door handle on the outside and attaching the rope to the banister. She had done the same thing to my door but also put a stepladder up against the door just in case

I tried to get out, in which case she would hear the ladder move and zip up the stairs.

Mr. Lawrence wasn't oblivious to the situation and sometimes snuck up chocolate bars. He'd slip them under the door in a clandestine way and mutter, "Don't tell your mother." Clearly he was scared of her as well.

So we couldn't even come out for the bathroom, Mum returned to the idea of setting buckets in our room as toilets. We were fed the bare minimum and rarely given water. Everything was a cruel game to Mrs. Lawrence, and she enjoyed the crueler ones immensely.

Intermittently, she'd torture us mentally by rattling and banging the doors, and other times she would also come in our rooms and beat us, generally about the head with her hands. She would always grab us around the back of the neck and bang our heads against furniture and walls, generally pushing us around violently.

There was no end in sight. Sometimes I prayed to God asking him to take me out of such misery. If that wouldn't work, I'd settle for school because as much as I hated it, it was an escape, a preferable hell.

※

One night Mr. Lawrence came home with a huge rectangular cage with him. We never expected to receive anything nice, so we looked at it with indifference. Something for the other kids undoubtedly. But when he walked in, his eyes twinkled and looked right at David and me.

"Here ya are," Mr. Lawrence said, setting the cage down. Inside were two large fluffy rabbits the size of a loaf of bread each. "Fluffy and Thumper, they're called."

I glanced at David whose jaw dropped. It really was for us! Mr. Lawrence wouldn't play a dirty trick on us, so we quickly accepted that these two little souls were ours to keep. As we cautiously bent down and scooped them in our little arms, we realized it was love at first sight. They were so defenseless but so naturally sweet and loving. Their noses wiggled as they sniffed us and came to know us as their parents. Apart from the love that David and I had for one another, the love we had for those rabbits was the only love we knew. We enjoyed giving them the care that we lacked; somehow that filled a hole inside me and put a smile on my face.

"Go feed your pets," Mum told us only a few days later. She shifted her eyes at us as we walked outside with a handful of their food, but we thought nothing of it as her heavy footsteps followed closely behind us as we opened the door.

When we walked to the cage, we could not believe what we saw: Fluffy and Thumper's heads were cut off.

At that moment, I felt like I had received a blow to the stomach. Tears stung my eyes as soon as I saw the pitiable scene before me, even thought I didn't process what had just occurred; it was too terrible. All I knew was that Mum did it; I just knew. She was laughing at the back door. Suddenly I felt my legs give out from under me, and I fell to my knees, letting the dam break loose. I sobbed and sobbed, David and I both did. How could anyone harm such innocent creatures?

When we collected ourselves, David and I carefully took their little bodies to the edge of the garden.

"Did you find a shovel?" I asked in a muffled voice. Each time I saw their headless bodies, convulsions shook me, and I had to cover my mouth lest I threw up.

David nodded. "I found one near the shed."

He squatted down and got to work, digging a deep-enough hole so the dogs couldn't get to the rabbits. His brow furrowed in concentration as he put every fiber of his being into creating the gravesite of our babies. Finally, when the mound of dirt behind the hole was about knee height, he announced, "They're ready."

I gently picked up the furry little bodies, so cold and limp. Looking up at the sky, I couldn't bear to look at their headless corpses any more than necessary. The convulsions turned to hot tears, which I allowed to freely roll down my face. We gently laid them both in the site and told them what good bunnies they were. The sight of them in a heap in a dirty hole was more than I could handle. Quickly I grabbed the shovel and buried them.

"We're so sorry she did this to you," I cried.

"C'mon, Ang," David said. "They're at peace now."

We walked into the house with our heads bowed low. There Mum waited for us. She looked down at us out of the corner of her eye and said, "I said that you would be sorry."

I did not understand how she could be so cruel. I knew it was going to be a long summer.

THEM AGAINST US

THE SOUND OF footsteps shouldn't be a child's greatest fear. Because I am locked in my room on many occasions, I always sat frightened in my room, wondering what would happen next. Whenever I heard someone coming up the stairs, I was afraid it was Mum coming to beat us again. Sometimes I was so hungry that every other complaint paled in comparison. Each day we were given the absolute minimum and were never allowed treats.

When we were downstairs eating with the family though, Mum scooped out large portions to her children right in front of David and me, while giving us portions that wouldn't feed a bird. Mum sat at the head of the table, and David and I were made to sit either side of her. If we spoke for any reason, she would turn her fork and hit the back of our hands or stab us with it. She never did anything of the sort to her own children, and they only laughed at our suffering. We helplessly glanced at Mr. Lawrence, hoping for an intervention, but he stared down at his plate of food and tried to block out the scene.

As a child, I shuddered and heaved just at the sight and smell of green beans. Each time they were served for dinner, Mum eyeballed me.

"You're not allowed to leave the table until you eat them all," she said on one particular occasion, scooping an extra large portion just for me. I stared at the insurmountable task and wondered if it might not be easier to climb a mountain.

David looked at me earnestly as if trying to channel his warning. Before dinner, he had said, "Put some on your fork, hold your breath, and then just swallow. Don't even chew 'em. Keep going like that."

I tried so hard to follow his advice, but it just wasn't working. My eyes watered, and my stomach rolled as the despicable green strings slid down my throat. Mum gritted her teeth more and more as she watched me, making me increasingly nervous. Finally she leaned over to me, grabbed my fork, and piled it high with green beans to force it into my mouth – scraping my gums with the utensil on the way in. I opened my mouth wider to avoid coming into contact with the fork, but she pushed the green beans all the way to the back of the throat, making me sick.

"That's disgusting! What's wrong with you?" she yelled.

She started to beat me on the head, in the face, and on the back with her plate even though I was still throwing up. Then she started banging my head on the table, and I thought I would pass out. My face was sweating profusely, and I felt unbalanced, like I'd fall and pass out on the floor. Finally I stopped throwing up, and she stopped beating me with her plate, which had broken while she was beating me.

"Eat it up," she snarled. It was clear to me that she didn't just mean the green beans, but the vomit as well. The three hours I spent trying to get the green vomit and beans up were among the longest of my life.

David wasn't immune to Mrs. Lawrence's violent force-feeding either. Sometimes we were so hungry that we were willing to take great risks to essentially stay alive. Tiptoeing downstairs to the cupboard in the dining room one night, David knew that the Lawrences zealously guarded a supply of Farley's Rusks. He took one and snuck it up to his bedroom with him. He tried eating it under his bed covers and, scared he would be heard, consciously avoided crunching them. Instead he sucked it so that it melted in his mouth.

David thought he hadn't been seen, but Amanda caught a glimpse of it and went downstairs. A few minutes later, Mum came upstairs. David could see her giant silhouette standing in his doorway and felt her anger radiating toward him.

"Get downstairs," she said in a deadly tone.

Petrified, David waited in the dining room for what seemed to be a very long period of time until she came in. Mum promptly went to the cupboard where the Farley's Rusks had been and took one out of the box. Suddenly she grabbed David, held him against the wall by his throat, and literally rammed the entire tin into his mouth. He started choking as the rusks split both sides of his mouth. After Mum got her pleasure, David was again sent to his room, and neither one of us were called for dinner that night.

Mom not only fostered us but also periodically looked after Nigerian children for a family that was going to school in London during the week. David always had to take care of these children throughout the night as if he were a single father, changing them and feeding them. The most that Mrs. Lawrence would do was prepare the bottles, but they were left with David because the babies were to become his responsibility so she could sleep through the night. If he couldn't get the babies to go back to sleep, she would rush into his room, grab the babies, shake them, and throw them in the cot as if they were dolls. Then David was next. Mum would beat him for not keeping them quiet.

Whenever I went into the kitchen during the day, I saw three poor little babies in high chairs all day, bawling their eyes out. Mum would never change their diapers, and I imagined they had terrible diaper rash.

"Shut up!" she screamed when she walked by them. She kicked at their chair and continued shouting at them, causing their faces to scrunch up and cry even more. If Mum fed them, she rammed the food into their mouth and nearly choked them, which never ceased to bring tears to my eyes. Having been in their position, I wanted to comfort them, so when David and I put them to bed, we would rock them, hug them, and shower them with kisses. We felt like their parents as we snuggled beside them and read bedtime stories.

"I hate when she does anything to them," David divulged one night. "I try to distract her from them."

"I'm surprised they aren't killed," I said sadly, looking at the tiny smooth face that was sleeping beside me. I wouldn't dream of waking them even if I wanted to. They were temporarily at peace.

David wrapped his body around one baby and held him in his arms. He rested his cheek against his head. We felt like the babies' makeshift parents. Though we lacked a great example of what a parent should be, love came naturally and flowed freely from us. As we loved the babies and took care of their pains, the same pains we had been suffering for years, the jagged hole in our hearts started to fill drop by drop.

* * *

At around eleven years old, we moved to a new house. We tried to view it as a new beginning, but we also couldn't help but wonder what horrors the new house had waiting for us.

One day, when I returned home from school, I went into the kitchen to get my usual chores done. Once I scrubbed and laid out the wet, clean dishes, I reached for the tea towel only to find it was sopping wet. I stopped in my tracks. *I'd get a beating if I dry with that tea towel because the dishes would still be wet when Mum checks on them.*

Sighing, I snuck upstairs to the cupboard to grab a new one even though it ran the risk of Mum beating me for getting a new one without asking. If I did ask, she'd still say no and beat me when the dishes were wet. She wanted absolutely any reason to hurt David and me. If she didn't have a good reason, she'd hurt us anyway. If she had a reason, the beatings were severer.

I couldn't win, and I knew it. Might as well get dry dishes out of it all.

Before I could even act on my plan of action, I heard footsteps coming up the stairs. My heart started pounding; I was hoping it wasn't Mum. I was so scared that I didn't even look around to see who it was. Then I heard the voice.

"What the hell do you think you are doing?"

Already trembling, I replied, "The tea towel downstairs was soaking wet so I came up to get a new one."

"Did you ask?"

"No." Obviously not.

I could tell she was getting closer because of the warm, moist breath on my neck. She then grabbed my hair and slammed my face into the boiler. My nose felt like it had been crushed, and it started to bleed. But of course she wouldn't stop there. Beating my head repeatedly into the boiler, she started pounding my head even harder when I begged her to stop.

"Please, no!"

She hit me even harder.

"Stop!"

Harder.

The pain was so excruciating I was unaware of anything else until Mum pushed me into my bedroom and slammed the door shut. I went to sleep that night struggling to breathe through my nose and stop the bleeding.

When I awoke the next morning, my face felt heavier than normal. I turned my eyes toward the pillow and gasped. It looked like a murder scene. On the pillow was a massive blood blot where my nose had dribbled, and it even spread to my sheets. Stumbling toward the mirror I saw that I had two black eyes and a nose so swollen I felt like an aardvark. My lips were cut inside and out, so I wondered whether Mum was going to lock me in my room instead of let me attend school.

When I went downstairs into the kitchen where Mum was, she saw my face and hers lit up with shock. Scooting her chair out, she shot up and said, "You have to tell them at school that you were pushed downstairs by some kids." She added that I should blame it on two boys in my class.

Without a better alibi and full of fear for what Mum would do to me if I told the truth, I gulped. I was so nervous to tell them the story at school because I knew that those two boys were going to get into trouble and then I would get picked on.

To appear caring, Mum took me to the doctors that afternoon to get me checked out. The doctor did not believe the story of me being pushed down the stairs and said I wouldn't have fallen on my nose.

"If you would leave the room for just a moment," he said, staring at Mum. She left the office, and he looked at me long and hard. "What's the truth of what happened?"

I started sweating under the scrutiny. I knew if I said anything she could kill me. Even though I thought about death and learned not to fear it, I worried she would kill David along with me. That wasn't fair to him.

"There were a couple boys at school," I began slowly, getting hotter under the intense gaze of the doctor. "They did it."

Though Nigel had joined the military, he came home sometimes to visit. The problem was that I was upstairs so much that I never knew when he was home because I was always isolated in my room. I found out because I heard Mum's heavy footsteps, and then the footsteps of someone else who sounded like he was wearing boots.

I turned to the door and saw Mum with a dog chain. Nigel dragged David in and threw him onto the spare bed. The next thing Nigel started whipping him with the chain. The chain creaked as it moved and lashed against David's skin. He let out a yowl, and as if that wasn't bad enough, Mum was punching him in the head.

"You're next," she added, locking her eyes on mine. I started crying; the screams were too much. I didn't understand. We hadn't done anything wrong, not that the facts ever mattered. I tried to get away, but Nigel stopped and grabbed me by my hair. He pulled my hair so I had to stare right at his relentless face. He bared his teeth like a dog as he yanked at my hair. Without warning he let go; I fell and hit my head on the floor, which hurt so badly I thought my brain shifted. In spite of that, I knew I had to get out. I stared at the window and, for a split second, thought my only escape was to jump out.

Nigel pulled me by one of my arms clad in my light blue nightdress and began to drag me across the floor. Then he picked me up and bent me over the single bed that was on the other side of the room. He positioned my hands so they were both on the bed and my forehead rested on the comforter. Both of my feet were on the ground, and I leaned forward in that vulnerable position. My mind swam until someone started lashing my back with the chain. It felt as heavy as bricks and bone breaking.

"Harder, do it harder!" Mum shouted. Her voice became shrill with excitement.

The chain connected with my hair, and I could feel it tangling my hair and pulling clumps from my scalp. I lay there, rigid, not daring to move or say anything. I lost count after fifteen, but the strikes went at least twice as long. Each strike felt like fire licking my back, only much heavier.

My back didn't sting. It didn't hurt. Rather, it was so mutilated that I felt like it was on fire. I started seeing splotches of color in front of my eyes before my vision went black. Mercifully, everything darkened to total blackness.

After that occasion, Mum would take every opportunity to incorporate an instrument of pain in our beatings.

Every day I prayed. Everything else seemed trivial in comparison to the need to stay safe.

"God, take David and me away from Mum. Why did you allow this to happen to us? Don't you love us? At this point all I want is an illness so I can go to heaven." As young as I could remember being, I pored over a billion reasons why God might be doing this to my twin and me. Eventually I settled on the fact we just must have been bad kids. Maybe we were so bad we didn't even know it.

The most unsettling possibility came from Mum. I had a birthmark on my cheek that I today affectionately call my coffee stain. Mum grabbed my arm one day and told me, "That's the mark of the devil! It means God will never love you and will *never* answer your prayers!"

My first instinct was indignant. There was no way that could be true; I hadn't done anything to earn "the mark of the devil." But at the same time, as I lay awake at night with sore body and preoccupied mind, my eyes wide open with fear, I wondered if it were true. God wasn't there for me. It seemed quite obvious. I prayed, but he didn't listen. Who knew the reason?

MONSTER WEDDING

THERE CAME A night when, from the confines of my room, I heard the announcement that Nigel and his girlfriend, Miranda, were engaged. The joyous sounds from Mrs. Lawrence's mouth were unlike any I had heard from her previously. Miranda was a beautiful, slim Irish girl with cascades of shiny brown curls. Her accent was cute, but what I loved most was how kind she was to us. I loved Miranda and was pleased she would be a member of the family, but she would never be able to get any of the hell to cease. Shrugging, I nestled under my thin sheet and went to sleep without another thought on the matter.

As the wedding got closer though, Miranda talked to David and me while we were gardening.

"Hello, lovelies. I'm here because Nigel and I were wondering if you'd like to come to Bournemouth Town Center with us today."

I dropped my hand shovel and stared at her like she was a mirage. "Really?"

"Yeah! Let's have a bit of fun." Miranda tossed back her brown wavy hair and shot us a grin.

David swiped his hand across his forehead to wipe the sweat, and I told Miranda we'd have to clean up, but we would definitely be willing to go. The one problem was Mrs. Lawrence.

"Don't worry about that," Miranda said. "Nigel took care of it."

Next thing we knew, David and I were on a bus ride down to Bournemouth Town Center. My nose was glued to the glass as the buildings whizzed by us and the scent of salt became increasingly present. When we got to the top of the tall hill, we could finally see the panorama of the beach and the famous Bournemouth Pier. Miranda's hands were folded in her lap, and she smiled as if she had a secret only she knew. Nigel sat beside her impassively.

The whole of Bournemouth is surrounded with beach, but there were two touristy ones: Bournemouth Beach and Sandbank Beach. I could only hope we would go because I had never actually felt the sand of the beach between my toes before.

"All right, time for the beach," Miranda said when the bus came to a halt. My heart skipped; it was like she read my mind! David and I unapologetically skipped off the bus and down the sidewalk as Miranda and Nigel trailed behind. We walked to the edge of the land, right by the ocean. The crashing and receding waves rejuvenated me in a way I never thought possible, and the breeze blew my blonde hair back affectionately. The water was so clear at Sandbank that I could see my toes wiggling at the bottom. When we made our way to Bournemouth, the water of the English Channel was much darker and the beach was pebbly. I loved it all.

"Didn't you guys want to go to the pier?" Miranda reminded us. That was undoubtedly the best part of Bournemouth, a landmark I had never yet seen! We nodded and let her lead the way.

It was a gorgeous seventy-degree day, so the pier was busy. Though we had to push past the masses of people, we were content. We stood by the railing of the pier and absorbed the scenery around us in case we wouldn't see it again for a long time. We were fascinated by the fact there was a pier theatre at the end of it.

"Here ya are," Miranda said, fishing out some coins from her purse. "Go get yourselves some candy floss and ice cream."

"Wow, thanks, Miranda!" I said. I was absolutely giddy. Whenever I look at big waffle cones like the ones we had that day, I can still smell the seaweed from Bournemouth Beach.

Though we lapped up our ice cream like it was our last meal, Nigel and Miranda took us to McDonalds. David and I had never been to a McDonalds and had no idea what to expect, but we rest assured that it would be good. It was mythical, like a child's first trip to Disney World. We couldn't have been more thrilled.

When we got the chicken nuggets and french fries, I looked at them like I had no idea what to do. I out-stretched my hand to a golden sliver and shakily put it in my mouth. My taste buds exploded at the salty, crispy snack.

"Oh my gosh, this is delicious!" I exclaimed.

David was too busy demolishing his Big Mac to add to my sentiments.

I was torn between wanting to eat my meal super quickly because it was so tasty or stretching it out to savor it. It was a dilemma unlike any I had before.

Nigel and Miranda sat opposite us and looked at each other knowingly. Then Miranda began to speak. "How would you feel about being part of our wedding?" she asked.

I froze. "Like how?"

"Well, I was thinking you could be one of my brides-maids and David could be a pageboy. Oh, Angie, it will be fun! You'll get your hair done nicely, and you can dress up…"

I didn't hear anything else. Conflicting feelings exploded within me. I felt special—terribly excited, really—but terrified too.

Why would she want me to be a bridesmaid? I thought. *I'm too ugly.*

I imagined Miranda standing in all her radiance with her tall, slender bridesmaids flanked on each side. Then I thought about awkward eleven-year-old me—

short, smelly, and unremarkable. I would stand out like a sore thumb. Everyone would laugh at me.

My heart pounded, and I couldn't think of any words in response to Miranda's thoughtful offer. Though I had no idea what paranoia was at the time, that's exactly what I felt. I felt I had never made any purposeful contribution to anything in life up to that point, but there it was!

"Th-thank you," I stuttered. *Wow, I can't believe it.*

"Excellent! How 'bout you, David?" she asked.

David's eyes were wide open, and he nodded almost imperceptibly.

Then human speech finally stopped escaping me, and a question arose. "Miranda," I asked carefully, "is Rebecca gonna be a bridesmaid too?"

She pursed her lips and shook her head.

Oh God! I thought frantically. *There is absolutely no way Mrs. Lawrence will let us do this now!* Even if Rebecca was a bridesmaid, I'm sure she wouldn't have let us be a part of the wedding. Still I couldn't help but grasp onto the tiny glimpse of my playing a role in Miranda's wedding—Miranda, who treated us better than our own mother and adopted siblings. That tiny glimmer of hope still glittered in my mind. Maybe, just maybe Miranda and Nigel could twist Mrs. Lawrence's arm. Nigel was her son after all, so maybe he had more influence that I even knew. I secretly hoped with all my might they could twist her arm.

On the bus ride home, I was vacant from my body as the realization crept in: Mum would never want any attention to be on us—not any good attention at least. She wouldn't mind if it was bad attention.

That night, I found out my most ardent desire was not to be.

"Miranda, dear, you don't want them in your wedding," Mrs. Lawrence said, spewing her upsetting news in an ironically polite voice.

"I thought it'd be nice," Miranda said slowly. She was unsmiling.

"No, no, don't. They are just being nice! They wouldn't want to actually be clean for a wedding. They're little piggies! They love being dirty. So nice of you, Miranda, but don't even worry about it."

"Well, okay. If you say so."

"Good. Anyway, Amanda, why don't you tell Miranda about your field trip?"

Everyone resumed dinner chatter as normal. And that was that.

Mr. Lawrence was scared of Mrs. Lawrence, and that was no secret. When I learned the news, I wondered if even Mrs. Lawrence's children and Miranda were scared of her too. Perhaps they didn't want to push the bridesmaid and pageboy issue and start a scene; maybe Mrs. Lawrence could be awful to her children if her despicable adopted children were involved in the argument, and they didn't wish to see that side of her. Hell, they could see what she did to us. Best not to set her off.

A few days before the wedding, we all traveled from Bournemouth to London. We were all to stay at Nigel and Miranda's flat to spend some time with Nigel and his new family and to run last-minute wedding errands. After we arrived, we all ventured out to Woolich because Mrs. Lawrence wanted to do some shopping. We went to the market where they sold fresh vegetables, fruits, and bread; then we went to Woolworth's and British home stores.

Mrs. Lawrence and Rebecca barreled through the doorway to the den after dinner. I heard Rebecca's voice first: "I swear it, Mum. That David stole a Mars Bar!"

I was in fetal position on the couch before I curled up even tighter and scrunched my eyes shut. David, steal? He wouldn't dare. My stomach churned uncomfortably for what was to come. This would cause nothing short of warfare.

"I wouldn't be surprised," Mrs. Lawrence snarled.

My eyes were closed, but I knew Rebecca was smiling smugly. She relished in our misery just as much as Mrs. Lawrence and Amanda. There was no way anyone would investigate to make sure this was actually true (which it wasn't).

"He's a thief! What'll you do about it?"

"I'll be giving Nigel a ring here in a few minutes. Better yet…Nigel!" Mrs. Lawrence barked out his name.

He scurried in from the other room. "Yeah?"

"Go give David a beating and take care of business like the good ol' days."

Nigel went running like a good boy and did as he was told—"like the good ol' days." Even though he was about to marry a sweetheart, he fell back into his old cruel game easily. My heart sank. I wished desperately that Miranda were with us at the flat rather than at her parents' house. My head started to hurt.

That beating he got that night…all I could hear were screams. The flat was two-story, and I heard the furniture scuffling across the floor upon impact. I heard the soft, blunt sound of a body against the floor. I heard the screams.

Up until that point, I had heard all kinds of screams. I remember instances where I screamed but never the sound. What remains branded in my mind to this day is the sound of David's screams that night. They were outrageous. I don't think I have ever heard him scream as loud as he did that day, not even during the incident with the pot of boiling water. Then there were the voices. Nigel's deep bellows corresponded with his huge size, which he undoubtedly used to his advantage.

Blinking back tears, I tried to remain calm though I thought I'd hyperventilate. I fixated on the phone on the table right beside the couch. A tiny, muffled voice inside me asked why I didn't have the courage to use it. I could've had Nigel and Mrs. Lawrence caught in their despicable acts against David. No, the reality of the matter was that once they were discovered, they may or may not receive a slap on the wrist. Then David and I would most certainly face death.

Everybody downstairs was just trying to make conversation like nothing was happening. I just covered my ears and sat there and cried. By then I did not care that Mrs. Lawrence would see me cry and probably pick on me too. It was pointless to save myself any longer; she was going to beat me for something, so it might as well have been for feeling true emotion. My poor twin was upstairs being flung around a room and beaten to death for something he did not do. The feeling inside me was wild, and I felt I was surely going mad.

Finally, I heard Nigel's heavy footsteps rattling the frames on the wall of the stairwell. "Mum, I didn't find any candy or wrappers up there," he said simply.

I was baffled as to why he would beat David up in spite of the fact there was no evidence against him.

"The greedy pig eat them," Mrs. Lawrence replied.

David's body was beaten black and blue, and he could barely walk. Since Miranda had been over at her parents while his beating occurred, it was not spoken of in front of her. I sincerely believed Nigel would not have beaten David if Miranda had been at home. Poor girl didn't truly know the man she would be marrying.

❧꙳❧

For the day of the wedding, Mrs. Lawrence got her way. I stared at myself in the full-length mirror in disbelief. She made me wear my baggy, plain navy blue school skirt. A huge safety pin kept it together so it wouldn't slip right off my hips. It fit like a Scottish kilt because it was one of Rebecca's skirts, so it was miles too big. Then on top I wore an oversized knitted black sweater with gray and white dogs on it. They even clashed with my beige-colored knee-high socks. Mrs. Lawrence never let me wear a belt. She used to get these big bags of potatoes that came in old, vile bags that were fastened together with brown twine. Instead of a belt, she would tie that twine around my waist.

"Ha, you look silly." She laughed, marveling at her handiwork. So not only were we bullied at school, but at home as well. I would bet my life that all she wanted was to cause us the utmost misery, and it was no different at Nigel's wedding.

I felt like an idiot.

Bitterly shifting my eyes over to the others, I saw Mrs. Lawrence's other two girls looking like pigs in makeup. Mum had their hair done up and curled. By contrast, she wouldn't let us shower and made sure David's and my hair was greasy for the wedding. It hung in strings by my pink national health glasses that were not attractive in any sense whatsoever. Miranda just couldn't believe it. I saw her looks of pity, but she wouldn't make a big deal about it with Mrs. Lawrence paying for much of the wedding.

The extent of Nigel's wedding for us was the ceremony and ten minutes of the reception. She would not let David and me in their wedding photos either.

"Oh, you don't want them in it," she said with a fake chuckle.

I didn't even argue. I didn't want my terrible look to be immortalized in photos.

After the reception just started, Mrs. Lawrence had us sent to bed.

PINNED DOWN

ONCE NIGEL MARRIED Miranda, he brought her over to spend time with the whole family. During that visit, I was particularly bitter and had made a tape recording while Mum was out.

Clutching the tape recorder close to my body so no one would hear, I said, "I hate Mrs. Lawrence, I love Mr. Lawrence, I hate Rebecca, I hate Amanda, I hate Nigel, but I love Miranda." Then I prayed, "Dear God, please let my real mum find David and me so she can come and get us."

Somebody always heard us no matter what precautions we took. This time it was Rebecca. She barreled into my room and pinned me up against the wardrobe, pushing me so hard that the mirror shattered behind me. She turned to me and bore her teeth.

"You are going to be in so much trouble!" she warned. Seeing my terror, she started smiling creepily and, with her open palm, kept smacking my forehead so that my head repeatedly banged against the wardrobe.

"I just can't wait till Mum comes home so I can show her what you've done!" She said after her final punch. With that, she calmly left the room and scooped up the tape recording on the way out.

My head was still spinning, and I started shaking nervously. When Mum came back, I had no doubt that the first order of business for Rebecca was to show her. Time was suspended as I waited in agony. The next thing I knew was the sound of the tape being played over and over again downstairs. Then Mum's muffled voice. Wincing, I waited for the inevitable.

Then Mum's footsteps.

She will kill me this time, I know it, I thought, scrunching my eyes shut. If nothing killed me before, then that day would surely be the day. The footsteps got louder and louder until, finally, she opened the door. Instead of coming toward me however, she went toward the lamp. I raised my eyebrows in disbelief as she took out the light bulb; then she grabbed the bucket she had sitting in the hallway and put it in the corner of my room. The door slammed.

The whole time I was more worried that she didn't beat me; the fact I could hear her tying the door handle was no comfort either.

Through those long, dark hours, I was not given food or water. I was confined to my room and saw no one until the following evening, when Nigel came in to my bedroom. He looked at me with a dangerous glint in his eye. In one swift movement, he grabbed my cassette player, lifted it up, and smashed it over my head. Falling forward to the floor, I literally saw stars.

"Why do you make her mad? You deserve this." He started to punch me in the face, but I could hardly feel it; I was numb. He was in such rage that I thought he was never going to stop. At that point, I did not care if he did kill me. I was ready to die and escape the everyday hell I endured. He was punching me with such force that I couldn't defend myself if I wanted to, and he wouldn't stop until his wife called up the stairs.

"Nigel! I thought we were leaving?"

He didn't even look at me as he swung his fist one last time and left the room.

My scalp was covered in lumps; I was weak, and my face was swollen to the point I couldn't even open one of my eyes. Lying on the floor in a ball, I was limp. A paranoid part of me worried I was paralyzed. I wanted my brother to hold me and to be close to me.

Looking up at my bed, I crawled over and thought I needed to rest. Once my head hit the pillow though, I couldn't move because of my fright. A voice told me that if I fell asleep, I wouldn't wake up. Then David would be alone. That's what brought the onslaught of tears, and I cried until I was so exhausted I couldn't help but fall asleep.

When I awoke in the morning, my lip puffed up and my eye wouldn't open. I had bruises all over my face and my body. I wanted to escape because then someone would *have* to believe me about the abuse, but there was no way out. The door was fastened shut, and the only other option was jumping from the window.

A short while after this incident, a lady from Kingsleigh School came around. I could hear her down by the front door as the hallway was directly under my bedroom.

"Thought I'd check and see why Angie hasn't been at school." With that, I lifted my ear toward the door to better hear the exchange, even though my head pounded with movement.

Mum flipped a switch that made her voice sound motherly and kind. "Angie has been sick all week, unfortunately."

She needs to come upstairs, I thought miserably. *Then she'd see.* Obviously she didn't. No one ever saw.

Later that day, David came home from school. We had a code together to make sure that each of us was okay. I was still locked in my bedroom. He came to the door and whispered through it. "Are you okay"?

Before he could do anything else, I then heard the sound of his footsteps running away. A short while later, I heard the door handle rattling and the rope being removed on the other side of the door. Mum stormed into the room, her fat jiggling like jelly with her anger. I stood up, and she came over to me, poking me in the chest. "What are you going to say?"

I had no clue what she was talking about. She stomped to the window and opened the window that I had my back toward. Returning to my front, she started to push me with all her might toward the window. My heart dropped into my stomach when I realized she intended to toss me out of the window.

"Turn around!" she yelled.

Closing my eyes I turned around nervously. When I opened my eyes I saw the window ledge pushing against my belly button. Panicking, I gripped that window ledge tighter than I had gripped anything.

Biting my lip, I looked out at the street, praying someone would walk by and notice me. I couldn't understand why no one was trying to find out who was screaming at the top of her lungs and crying out for help as if they were about to take their last breath.

The next thing I heard was David shouting. Mrs. Lawrence didn't seem deterred initially, but suddenly, I felt her cold grip around my calves. Then my body sloped downward. My jaw dropped—she was trying to tip me out of the window!

"Help!" I screamed. All I could see was the concrete path below me.

"Let her go! Let her go!" David yelled. His pleas didn't make a difference; I was hung upside down outside the window and scared for my life. Closing my eyes, I thought, *I'm really going to heaven now*. I closed my eyes. That calmed me until I remembered that David was alone. He had to go with me! I never wanted to be without my brother! If David had to stay here with Mum, she would be mean to him for the both of us.

The next thing I knew, I was being pulled up and over the window. It was only then I turned around and realized that David was standing in the bedroom holding a large kitchen knife. All color drained from Mum's face; she truly looked like a ghost. For once in her life, she said nothing. Shakily moving my head toward David, I was blown away: he finally cracked. He had no fear. He had a wide stance, pointed the knife right at Mum, and just said, "I've had enough."

Mum then walked out of the room without saying or doing anything. She just left.

David suddenly dropped the knife with a clatter and ran toward me, hugging me like never before. We stood there for a few minutes holding each other and saying nothing.

Although Mr. Lawrence never protected us from Mrs. Lawrence, being a timid man himself, we came to depend on his presence anyway because the abuse was never as bad when he was around. We couldn't blame him if he wanted to escape though because that's exactly what we wanted to do if it were at all possible.

But then he really did leave.

Once he left for a couple of weeks, and the second time for a month. The second time was after we had moved to a new house on Nutley Way. We didn't know why he left and wished with all our might that he would because we were confined to our bedrooms. All day long I sat by the window, hoping to soak up every ray of sunlight I could and to see Mr. Lawrence walk up the garden path.

God, why did he leave us? Does he not like us after all? It was maddening to sit inside the same four corners all day long. David and I missed him so much. We felt like we lost our one ally, and even our ally didn't seem to care about us enough to do anything about our wretched abuse.

That day, even without knowing anything about the situation, I stared at the cobblestones on the garden path for so long that everything went fuzzy like a watercolor painting and wished Dad had strength enough to help us. Why on earth wouldn't he support us? If he wouldn't tell her to stop, couldn't he have whisked us away to live with him?

A MIRACLE

WITHOUT EXPERIENCING SERIOUS discussions about God, Jesus, or the devil, I had an innate sense of them for as long as I could remember.

My "coffee stain" birthmark—a tiny little mark by my mouth—was Mrs. Lawrence's opportunity to make a cruel joke. She saw me pray on numerous occasions and outright laughed at me.

"God isn't listening to you! You have the mark of the devil. You're completely unlovable!"

I kept my eyes squinted shut and continued whispering to God.

"Might as well stop praying because he will never answer *your* prayers!"

I've always known Jesus, and I attribute that to one of God's many miracles. I've always spoken to God as if I were speaking to anybody else but with the utmost respect. When I'm mad at him, as I was at that moment, I tell him, "Why, God? Why? Stop teaching me these lessons. Give me a break."

I knew Jesus came to me in the mirror when I was younger. Every fiber of my being wanted to scream out against Mrs. Lawrence and tell her how hopelessly wrong she was, that God was especially present with the downtrodden. But because I was a kid with no true understanding of Scripture or religion, her words started to permeate my mind.

Maybe she's right, I thought. *God isn't answering any of my prayers.*

I surveyed my room, unadorned and ratty with the oldest bed sheets that she would never wash. I didn't even have a functioning light. Night after night, I was sent to that pitch-black space and began to wonder if God damned me as a creature of darkness.

Sometimes I was sick with anger. Fundamentally I could not believe I was worthy of my life. I thought back to when David and I took care of Fluffy and Thumper and how we routinely showered the Nigerian babies with love. There was no way that loving creatures as ourselves only amounted to cursed filth. Plus, I could not give up on God. If I did, then all I had in the world was David.

"If I really am in the devil's grip, please take it off of me," I begged tearfully during my prayers. I sat at the edge of my bed and firmly held my hands together. "Take the devil off of me so you can love me instead."

At that time in my life, I didn't know any better. The devil was a fantasy-like creature with orange cat-like eyes and huge red horns, but the most unsettling part for a child as myself was that I truly thought the devil could beat God. If God's love couldn't overpower the mark of the devil, then why wouldn't it be that way?

I didn't know at the time that God speaks to us in subtle ways. It was just a matter of paying attention.

When David and I exited the school to begin walking home weeks later, a man was passing out fliers with a red icon at the top. He presented us one with a gentle smile, so we shrugged and accepted it. Why not? We walked and read the flier. "The Salvation Army," it read.

The Salvation Army was based in Winton in Bournemouth and was approximately a ten-minute drive from Bournemouth Center. Apparently at that time, they started going to the smaller towns to recruit kids to come to Sunday schools. That's what they were doing that day.

When we arrived home, David and I discovered the other kids got the same fliers.

"I think it sounds fun, Mum," Rebecca said. She put her book bag down by the couch and flopped by her mother. "I hear there's lots of singing and dancing, lots of kids my age."

"All right, Rebecca, enough pleading. You can go."

She clapped her hands gleefully and planned to go the very next evening.

We didn't think anything of it or hoped one way or another. The only thing in our future was a soiled kitchen floor and laundry. Some ground beef had been sitting out all night, and I squashed a cockroach with a balled-up paper towel. My only satisfaction would be preventing more bugs from trailing in to eat the leftovers cemented in the pot.

So that was the contrast in our lives: Rebecca attended the Salvation Army Youth Group while David and I tended to the house. This carried on for a few weeks until our house received a ring.

"Hello?" David answered. He had a dishtowel over his left shoulder. "May I ask who is calling?" His eyes reflected confusion.

Thankfully, in this case, Mum snatched the phone from him. "This is Mrs. Lawrence speaking…yes. Oh." Her countenance darkened. "Yes. Well, I doubt they will want to. But I can try."

She quietly hung up the phone. "Rebecca's youth group heard about you two. You're going."

And it was as simple as that.

David and I went along with Rebecca that Sunday with no idea what to expect. We were silent in the car the whole way there and wondered if Rebecca would make it another place where we were tortured and taunted. I stared down at my knee-length blue skirt and hoped people could look past it—just once.

"Have fun," Mrs. Lawrence said after dropping us off, only looking at Rebecca. Then she drove away, leaving a trail of exhaust that blew in our faces.

There's a saying to expect the worst and anything more is a pleasant surprise. We went to the midmorning program and walked in with our breaths held. As it turned out, the Salvation Army was great—no, amazing.

"Hello there," a man with watery, kind eyes said. He instantly greeted us and stuck by our side as Rebecca skipped off to her friends. "I haven't seen you two around here! I'm Paul. What are your names?"

"David," he replied spoke in a chipper voice. Unlike me, David could more easily detach from our family life and thrived off of nice human interaction whenever he could grasp it. He had more friends at school than me, though we were still taunted for our smell and appearance.

"And you?" Paul looked at me and smiled.

"Angie," I squeaked.

"Well," Paul said, "we are happy to have you both. We have a few other new kids over here I'd like you to meet." He motioned for us to follow him to the rows of chairs in the middle of the room. Toward the back sat the other new kids. They were wide-eyed like me, and somehow that comforted me.

Once the program started, Paul and the band commenced worship. As it turned out, he could play the guitar and sing. Many of the other children contributed their voices and instrumental ability to lead the rest of us in the audience.

There was something in that room that day that finally soothed my troubled spirit. Normally, when I was in the midst of people, I couldn't get enough air and constantly looked toward the doors. Each hour at school would be wrought with anxiety. But there, in that room, there was an essence of pure comfort in the air. The other kids smiled at me; my acceptance was never a question. Not one person commented on my clothes or sneered. I finally breathed, maybe for the first time in my entire life.

When the speaker read from the Scripture, he had my rapt attention:

> The Lord is close to the brokenhearted
> and saves those who are crushed in spirit.
>
> —Psalm 34:18 (NIV)

I knew it made sense. All along I knew. I just wondered if Mrs. Lawrence were correct—an unsettling thought—but now I had the scriptural proof that God really did care. That was all I needed.

The Salvation Army had singing company choir on Monday nights. On Sundays there were three services: a service in the morning, another service in the afternoon, and a final service in the evening. If nothing else, we would sing on Sundays and had Sunday school followed by Bible study. If Mrs. Lawrence wouldn't drive us, then they had a minibus to come pick us up. Becoming involved in that organization is when I was able to start tolerating my life. That's when I calmed down. That's when I wanted to stop dying. That's when I knew that, eventually, life would improve.

The minute I can, I'm out of here, I thought. *She cannot tie me down. I'm going to leave school and the house, and there's nothing she can do.*

When Mum asked how we liked it, we made sure to play the part of bullied, unlikable children. After all, we normally were. I stuck my lower lip out and shifted my eyes downward. "It was kind of boring."

"The other kids were mean," David said.

"Why do you think I care?" Mum cut in. "Stop complaining. You're going!"

David squeezed my hand when we walked upstairs. We knew we were set. The best part was that Rebecca never said a peep against us. She saw us smiling and laughing but never even told Mum we were clearly fibbing. I truly knew at that point that God was answering my prayers and working through Rebecca. If it wasn't for her uncharacteristic desire to go to a church organization, who knew where David and I would be?

That's what I call God's big miracle in our lives. He had to work through Rebecca to get through to Mrs. Lawrence because if Rebecca didn't go, we wouldn't be going. I'm glad we had the wisdom to say we thought it was boring because there was no way she would have let us go otherwise.

That night, for one of the first times in my life, I sat at the edge of my bed on my knees and thanked God. I must have said thank you twenty times for allowing me to better know him and to finally find purpose in my life. There was finally a light at the end of the tunnel.

For David and me, simple things like getting a hug was like winning the lottery. Whenever we went into the Salvation Army Sunday school, we became millionaires. So many people were giving us ample love. Before, it was such a scarce concept that David and I could only give to each other. As soon as we walked in though, we were in the middle of a bowl of love.

Sometimes it was still extremely jarring. David and I didn't trust most people at all, especially not adults. They only ever failed us. It took us a long time to be able to be affectionate with anybody.

A lady named Hilary walked up to me and gave me a hug one day. The first thought in my mind was, *What do you want?* Then *What are you going to do, why are you being so nice?* That was especially true of me. I was standoffish and only gave Hilary a weak pat on the back instead of hug.

She pulled away and gave me a dazzling, genuine smile. "Have you and Dave ever thought of coming to singing company on Monday?" she asked.

"What's that?" I said.

"Well, we just come together and sing! It's more music-oriented worship. I see you and David really enjoy music, so I think you should give it a go."

"Okay. Thanks, Hilary," I replied with a shy smile.

She gave me an affectionate tap on the shoulder. "Call me Billy. All my friends do."

Billy was always exceptionally kind. David and I never had much attention paid to us, so we could only watch in awe as she spoke to us with respect. When we finally did join on that Monday night, she greeted us with a hug. More and more, I started to realize that people maybe could be nice without expecting anything in return.

"Let me know how you like it," she told us before it started.

Like it? She should've asked how much we loved it. We did. We absolutely loved it. Billy looked at us with twinkling eyes as we poured ourselves into the music. It renewed me from the inside out, like the feeling I had on rare occasions when I just awakened from a good night's sleep without any sore places on my body. By the end of it, she rushed over to us, smiling like she had a secret.

"What would you two think about doing a duet?" she asked us. David and I froze in disbelief because we had never been asked to do anything really nice.

"Well?" she asked with a laugh like a bell. "I'll work with you two for a month and make sure you're up to pace."

"That's not a problem," David said. "I'm in."

"Me too."

"Excellent!" she said. "Let's start Saturday. I'll take you two for lunch after. My husband Nori would love to meet you."

And she did. Her husband and kids took extra care and special interest in us. They were all lovely people who had a genuine concern for others. Long past our duet, Billy kept in touch with David and me and made sure we stayed up to date on youth activities.

Around our birthday, there was a youth trip to the nearby water park. David and I had never been to anything so fun, so when they showed us pictures from years passed, we were all but drooling.

"How are we going to pay?" I whispered to him. I saw David's jaw fall open with the horrid realization. He turned to me. "We have to find a way!"

"Maybe we can ask Billy if we can work for extra cash?"

We could barely listen to the sermon after that. It was a steady hum in the background as I rummaged my brain for options. I didn't know what would happen if we couldn't go. On one hand, I was accustomed to disappointments, but the last thing I wanted was to miss out being with all the people I loved.

Finally, it ended. I bolted to Billy immediately. "We don't have the money to go!" I blurted out. "Is there a way we can earn the money?"

Billy looked at me like I was crazy. "It doesn't matter if you can pay or not. We've got ya covered. Your birthday is coming up, isn't it? It's my gift."

We could barely believe our ears, but we didn't say a word against it!

The day was a blur of happiness that was so rare for us. They bought us ice cream, which was like a drug on our tongue. Such sweet flavors were entirely absent from our palate. We even got hot pink candy floss.

"Oh my gosh," David said, closing his eyes as he trailed his nose along the string.

"What?" I asked.

"It just smells so good! I've never smelled anything like it. Here, try." He gave me some, and my eyes popped open with the realization: it smelled *so* good. It might've been the best smell ever.

"Aah! Give me some more!"

David and I were two addicts. When we finally got outside our little bubble of ecstasy, all the other kids looked at us with raised eyebrows. One even asked us, "Why you makin' such a big deal out of candy?"

"We're not allowed to eat it," was all I said.

Though the water park was fun, I was enraptured by candy. We passed by the window of a gift shop, and I saw lollipops the size of my head. I had never seen such huge ones! I would have been satisfied with a little one. My next mission would be to grab one of those sometime in my life.

Christ was all the family I had apart from David, and it was the best gift in the world to finally know him. He was the bright light in my life. Though I knew I would remain deathly afraid of Mrs. Lawrence, I felt an unprecedented inner strength as I came to know Christ more and more through the Salvation Army. He soothed me in my toughest times, and as alone as I felt, I logically knew I never was. Even when I wasn't at Sunday school, I was coming to know the man who lived inside my heart very intimately.

If God is for us, who can be against us?

—Romans 8:31 (NIV)

DARKEST BEFORE DAWN

CHRIST WAS MOST assuredly in my life. Once I started regularly attending Sunday school and choir, I knew that it was miraculous that I always knew about him. Now, thankfully, I knew he was on my side. Often I murmured Bible verses to get myself through difficult days. Make no mistake: there were no shortage of them, and I wasn't magically positive about my circumstances. Especially once puberty hit.

When I started my period, I had no idea what was going on. I stared blankly at the rusty red stain with no idea how to process it. The possibilities flew through my mind: Was I hurt? Was I dying? I felt okay, at least, but who knew. Mrs. Lawrence certainly had never spoken to me about such things, so I had no idea what was happening.

When I came home, I was perturbed. I hardly noticed Mrs. Lawrence watching television with her friend Val Lewis; I trudged upstairs to my bedroom to be alone. Peeling off my underpants, I changed into a new pair and then put on my nightdress. I thought that maybe my blood flow would slow down. *Maybe it was just a fluke*, I reasoned.

Within a couple hours, I felt blood saturating the nightdress. I turned my bum toward the mirror and saw blood all over the back. That's when my eyes welled up and the "what ifs" assaulted my mind. I sat upstairs on my own feeling scared and becoming progressively more hysterical. If I told Mrs. Lawrence, I doubt she would care or do anything. However, it got to the point I just had to do something because doing nothing while bleeding was maddening.

My door flew open, and I zipped downstairs. "There's blood on me," I said, out of breath. I blinked back tears.

Without a word Mrs. Lawrence jumped from the sofa, yanked the front of my nightgown, and dragged me into the kitchen.

"Take off your nightdress," she demanded. I did immediately and stood there naked as she started to fill the sink with hot water and salt. As she grabbed the nightdress from me, Mrs. Lawrence repeated, "You are a dirty bitch" over and over. She threw the nightdress in my face and started rubbing the stained area all over my chin and cheeks.

Lewis, who was standing by the doorway, even joined in. "You *are* dirty! You should know what to do with this."

Mrs. Lawrence got hold of my hands, pushed them into the water with the nightdress, and made rubbing motions. She finally let go and kept me scrubbing until the tops of my fingers, the area in between my fingers, and my knuckles started to bleed.

"Rub that hard to get this nightdress clean," she said. "And if your brother sees you naked, I'm going to give you what for!"

Unbeknownst to me, David had seen me standing there naked. If he had, I didn't know if I could take the paranoia.

❧❧

The next day at school, I spoke to the school nurse about starting my period. She was much more understanding and acted like it was no big deal. She nodded and smiled. "It's something that happens to all women," she said. "It's just your body's way of showing you can now have a baby."

Warm relief spread through me the more we talked about it.

"All you have to do is use tampons or towels," she said. "And it will only last about five to seven days once a month."

I hated the feeling like I had wet my pants, and pads seemed like a diaper, so I asked more about tampons.

"Yes, this is how you use them," she said, grabbing one as a prop. "Lots of girls use them."

"All right, I want to try those," I said. The nurse gave me a few until I could buy some of my own.

When I got home, I stupidly told Mrs. Lawrence. She slammed down the spoon she was using to stir the stew and shouted at me. "You like stuff in your hole, don't you? You like stuff in your hole! You're a slut!"

I walked up to my room looking shell-shocked. Sinking onto my bed, I lay there staring at the ceiling until David poked his head into my room.

"What's going on?" His voice changed and made my face split into uncontrollable laughter. He was doing his Donald Duck impression!

"What you laughing about?" he demanded, getting my face. I laughed until tears formed in my eyes as he continued. "You're crazy!"

He impersonated Donald Duck until spit flew from his mouth, and I couldn't breathe. David knew me; he knew when all I needed was a laugh, and no one could make me laugh like him.

❦

The normal routine followed. On a whim, Mrs. Lawrence sent me to my room, put a rope around my door, and locked me in the bedroom.

The period situation had unnerved me and caused something within me to snap. All I wanted was the commiseration of other girls. The nurse made periods sound like I crossed the threshold of womanhood, but I was still beaten and punished like a little disobedient child.

At school, I made the conscious decision to open up to the two nicest girls I knew, Lisa and Danielle. As far as I recalled, they never made fun of me. Thankfully I was getting to an age where everyone was maturing and bullying was infrequent. Our mutual involvement in the Salvation Army choir was working wonders on us too; David was becoming more of a social butterfly because he learned to detach and muffle the trauma of home life. As for me, I was a withdrawn girl who opened up to a scant few. But Lisa and Danielle sat with me at lunch most days, and we even sat together at Sunday school. They were naturally sweet and gentle people I was glad to have met.

At the playground that afternoon, we sat on the swings and lazily rocked ourselves back and forth. My fists were balled in the pockets of my too-big wool coat, still raw from washing the nightdress. I bit into my lip and peeled off a flake of chapped skin. Lisa chattered beside me, but I couldn't hear her until she said, "Angie, what's up?"

I looked up at her face, creased with worry, and I broke down. "There's something I need to show you," I blurted out. "Come here." Moving aside my jacket, I lifted up my shirt and showed them mottled bruises on my ribs. That caught their attention. Next I glanced around to make sure no boys were nearby, and I lifted my skirt. There was *the* bruise. The big one.

They gasped but said nothing. Lisa looked less fazed than Danielle. Looking at me without emotion, all she said was, "I know."

Later that night I lay awake and thought about Lisa's comment. It told me two things. One, Lisa could see signs of my abuse without me having to say anything, two, she hadn't said anything about it because she was too scared or didn't care enough to act. That told me that maybe my other classmates and teachers knew. I supposed my abuse was more obvious than I even realized. But the fact no one had reached out or even investigated Mrs. Lawrence overwhelmed me with a deep sadness I wouldn't be able to shake for a long, long time.

After school the next day, I walked into the house and into the living room. Mrs. Lawrence was sitting in there, and her head popped up when she saw me. She snapped up, grabbed the nearest mug, and shouted, "You f——ing b——!"

My mouth fell open, but I dodged the mug. I sprinted from the living room to the kitchen, but she followed. Veering to the left, I started to run upstairs. Even though Mrs. Lawrence was a fat lady, she caught me while I was bolting upstairs and grabbed my school jumper.

I was in for it.

She grabbed hold of my hair and started dragging me upstairs. There were no words for the abject agony I felt as my body hit each stair; I thought I'd scream from the carpet burn. She continued pulling me by my jumper and screamed, "You are a big-mouth b——! You are a liar!"

Still holding my hair, she yanked me over the last step and dragged me to the bathroom. Once inside, she released me, and I flopped on the floor. I could see her filling up the bath. A cold, sick feeling washed over me. I knew she was going to do something to me, but I didn't know what. I could only guess as to how she'd convert a bathroom into a torture chamber. My anxiety immobilized me; I didn't have the courage to run away. I helplessly looked on.

Mrs. Lawrence then turned to me and dragged me over to the bath so that I was on my knees and leaning against it.

"You're dead."

Next thing I knew I felt her fingernails digging into my scalp and steaming hot water washing over my head. Each second ticked by with the scalding water stinging my face.

Then she yanked me out. My wet hair hung in strings over my face, making it difficult to breathe. Abruptly she dunked my head back in, continuously in and out. I really thought I was going to die.

Maybe it wouldn't be so bad, I thought. Strangely, that idea calmed me. I could join Jesus in heaven. I would escape this hell. I could not see anything else for me.

But it was as if Mrs. Lawrence knew I accepted that possible fate. I didn't know how much time had passed, but she stopped. Without a word, she stomped out of the bathroom.

Somehow I managed to crawl into the bedroom, lying on the floor and not wanting to move. My face was stinging, and it even hurt to breathe. I was still in my school uniform, which was soaking wet. I lay on the floor, unmoving, until I heard Mrs. Lawrence slamming the door and locking it.

And so my captivity began.

Mrs. Lawrence left me in the bedroom for days. No one came to visit, but I was occasionally bought food. The bucket was still in the corner of my room to use as a toilet, and my light bulb was removed. That was my living situation for three days—and I knew it was three because I counted. I had all the time in the world to pay attention to the light and the sun's position in the sky.

After the third day, the door opened, and David came into my room. I was too dead to the world to even react verbally; my eyes slid down to the plate in his hands. There sat a sandwich.

Strange, I thought. *He has never sent me food before.* He quickly left it with me and ran out; I guessed he feared Mrs. Lawrence's reaction. Picking up the sandwich, I lifted it to my mouth and took a bite. As soon as I did, my face crinkled in disgust. It didn't taste right at all, so I opened it up to see why. The answer was quickly apparent: it looked like someone chewed shrimp sweets up and spat them onto the liver sausage. Flesh-pink lumps sat in a heap, coated in a film of saliva.

The next memory I have was lying on the bunk of my bedroom. I looked over dully as Mrs. Lawrence came in and turned on the lights. She was wearing a knee-length white dress with black patterns on it, which revealed her round calves. Something was in her hand. Squinting, I saw that it was a broom.

"Get out of bed," she said. Her voice was deadly calm. It scared me worse than her screaming because it was so rare.

On the opposite side of the bedroom was a single bed for when she privately fostered other children, like the Nigerians. She told me to move to that one.

"Now pull up your nightdress and lean forward on the bed."

My eyes darted back and forth. She had a completely different tone I had never heard her use before, and this was a new request. I didn't have any undergarments on because she never let me wear them to bed. She was still so calm, serene even. I had no idea what she was going to do. My stomach felt weighed down by cement as I wondered.

Still, I did what she told. My nightdress sat halfway up my back.

"Part your legs," she said simply.

At that stage, I knew she was going to do something terrible. I heard a scraping sound against the metal frame of the bunk bed.

"Move to the left of the wardrobe."

At that point I was shaking like a leaf.

The next thing I felt was the handle of the broom brushing against my skin; I saw it move downward out of the corner of my eye before my eyes darted to the quilted pattern on the bed spread. I focused on the sewn roses while my heart pounded against my chest. All of a sudden, I felt a sharp pain inside my bottom, so tight and so unbelievably painful. I thought I had to poo. Next I felt her pulling the handle out. I sharply inhaled; my bottom clenched around it because I was so tense.

Mrs. Lawrence kept pulling it out then jamming it in harder and harder each time. As she gained momentum, she started shouting. "Do you like that? I told you, you are a slut, and this is what sluts get." She stabbed the handle inside me. I screamed. The pain was unimaginable, unable to be strung into words.

She put the handle in at least fifteen times. In the end, I couldn't take it anymore. My whole body was drenched in sweat, and my stomach rolled. I clasped my slick hands together, but they slipped apart. Gulping my nausea down, I tried to shut my legs together but couldn't manage. The nausea increased tenfold, but I only vomited words. "Just kill me and get it down with!" I finally screamed. "I can't take it anymore! Why? *Why?*"

Then just like that, she stopped. She yanked the broom out from inside me and turned. She exited the room without a word.

Over the next few days, Mrs. Lawrence repeated the broom incident approximately three times, each done exactly the same as the first time. There was nothing I could do. If I would go against her, she would only hurt me in other ways, so I just gave up and let her do what she wanted to do.

As I sat curled up in bed trying to ignore the pain in my bottom, I knew something within me changed. Of course, I would never be the same after Mrs. Lawrence's abuse, but there was something so utterly dirty and violating about the broomstick incident. Something died in me that day. I erected walls around me ever since I was a child, but after my rape, I erected walls larger and stronger than anything prior.

My bottom half was desecrated. Irrevocably. Completely.

In those terribly lonely moments in the darkness of my room, I stared out at a starless sky. Memories floated back that I had repressed. Already numb, I couldn't even be horrified when I remembered an experience from long before.

Mrs. Lawrence had been out with her friends all day. Mr. Lawrence used to smoke Old Hogan, and since she was gone, David and I wanted to see what it tasted like. He was out in the backyard tending to the cabbages anyway, which gave us a perfect chance.

We snatched some of his tobacco and took his papers. Clumsily, we rolled up the crackly paper and the pungent plant into rolled-up cigarettes, which was actually quite fun.

"How's it look?" David asked.

"Well, it's really fat," I replied. "Sort of like a cigar."

We shrugged, and David tucked it into his pocket—just in time, because Mr. Lawrence came back in to watch the horse races on television.

"Can we go play outside?" David asked.

"Yeah, sure," he said. His eyes never left the television; the horse races were his favorite.

David and I pushed the door open and sat on the steps. Extracting a light and our makeshift cigarette (or cigar, rather), we lit it up and watched the swirls of entrancing gray smoke dissipate into the air. My heart leapt; I felt so adult holding the cigarette.

Murphy's Law was the rule of our lives: Mrs. Lawrence returned home and caught us smoking it.

"What is this?" she boomed. She stood at the doorway with her hands on her hips. Deer in the headlights, I had the cigarette in my hand and had just blown out a puff. David looked at me in alarm. Instinct took over.

"It was my idea," I blurted out. There was no need for David to get in trouble too; I couldn't bear seeing him hurt.

She nodded. "Right then. Get in your room. I'll be teaching you a lesson."

When she came upstairs, she had rolled cigarettes of her own. It was a similar ordeal to the broomstick incident, which is why it slipped from my repressed memories. She told me to take my pants off, and she lit the cigarette on fire. I screamed as she dug it in my privates.

After I remembered that other instance of sexual abuse that night after the first broomstick situation, I found myself feeling the cigarette scars. It was smooth and hairless—and would always remain so. My devastation was oppressive to the point I couldn't even produce tears. I was just a child when she burned me with cigarettes, but as I aged, I saw it for what it really was: Mrs. Lawrence's permanent mark on me. It was a branding that would always remind me of my upbringing in hell.

THREE CHANCES

THROUGH ATTENDING THE Salvation Army in Winton, David and I learned that not every human being was terrible. In fact, there were extremely nice people in the world. The Salvation Army was nothing but hospitable and kind to us, and the people in its youth groups were all accepting. Luckily David and I befriended people that embodied its values in the Simmons family. Sometimes the Simmons dropped by our house to pick us up or take us to choir.

"Angie! David!" Mrs. Lawrence shouted from downstairs. "Get your lazy bums down here!"

My face turned hot and pink as I realized Ms. Freda Simmons was waiting downstairs and had heard the way she spoke to us. The last thing I wanted was for one of my few allies to take on Mrs. Lawrence's perspective of us. Nervously buttoning my cardigan, I slinked downstairs and wouldn't look at Freda in the eye.

"Don't stay out too late and don't you dare act like a slut," Mrs. Lawrence said. No matter how many times she said it, the s-word cracked into me like a whip.

"Yes, Mum."

Freda turned her head as she led us outside; only then would I look up at her expression. Her eyes flashed suspiciously and she grimaced. "Come along," she said in a gentle tone that ill fit her expression. I heard Mrs. Lawrence slam the door behind us, and only then did she look down.

"If you ever need anything, please call me, dear," she said softly.

"I don't have your number," I murmured.

Freda nodded and opened the car door for us. Once we were all in, she grabbed a receipt from inside her purse and scrawled her number on it in bright blue ink. "There," she said. "Keep it handy."

I slipped it in my breast pocket and swore it would stay there. With Mrs. Lawrence's unpredictability, Lord only knew when I would need it.

The weekend after the broomstick incident, I managed to sneak out of the house and run to the phone box at the end of the street. I threw open the door, extracted the paper with her number, and smoothed it out. In that moment I must have recited the number twenty times to commit it to memory just in case the paper were to become damaged. Life had become unbearable in a matter of seven days, and I had to make sure I could rely on myself to call my saviors.

"Simmons residence?" It was Freda.

"Freda! I have to get out of here. Please, please come help."

"What's going on?"

Without divulging too many details, I said I had it with Mrs. Lawrence and continued begging for help. Because she was already suspicious, she told me she'd be over as soon as she could.

Within the hour, Mrs. Simmons and her two daughters, Theresa and Claire, appeared at the house. Unfortunately the whole house was there—Amanda, Rebecca, and Mr. and Mrs. Lawrence—and, of course, David. Mrs. Lawrence was aghast and kept looking at them and back at me venomously.

"The bloody hell's going on?" she demanded.

"Angie called saying she was in trouble and needed our help," Freda said.

I saw fire in Mrs. Lawrence's eyes. Her deadly growl turned into violent shouting. "This is ridiculous! This little troublemaker here does anything she can to stir up a fuss! She's a bad, *bad* kid!"

With the Simmons's presence there, I felt no intimidation. David peeked in from the den and silently rooted me on. I nodded at him before turning back to her. "Oh yeah?" I challenged. "Then how do you explain David's burns?"

"Burns?" Freda asked, blinking rapidly.

"Just one example of her evilness," I said. I began the story of the boiling pot of water and told every last detail, which wasn't difficult considering that scene played out like a horror movie in my mind every night. Freda, Theresa, and Claire's faces contorted in disgust. I knew I had done what I needed to.

"Freda, she is evil. She is evil!" I emphasized at the end. I had no idea where my strength came from. The promise of a better life must have invigorated me.

"Yes," Mrs. Simmons said, faintly nodding her head. "Yes, you can come with us. *Please* come with us."

"Take her away then!" Mrs. Lawrence shouted.

I didn't even turn around as I followed Freda and her girls outside.

❧❀❧

Mrs. Simmons walked as if she were in a daze after the news, but around me, she was nothing but smiles. "You're welcome here as long as you need to be," she told me. Her two-bedroom house was small but warm and cozy with love. The added bonus was that I was able to play with her daughters whenever I wanted, like a continual sleepover. Sometimes all three of us fell asleep in one bed after chatting way too late. The girls were awkward at first with the information, but they pretended like it didn't happen shortly afterward. It was easier for them, and I didn't mind—it was easier for me too.

School was much more tolerable once I was allowed to shower. I turned the water as hot as it would go and let it wash away any lingering filth from Mrs.

Lawrence's house. As I ran my fingers through my wet hair, I told myself it was time to start life anew and to forget Mrs. Lawrence as much as possible.

Once I cleaned up and wore clothes that fit, people stared at me as if I were a new girl. It improved when I tried contacts. As pleased as I was to be clean, I was unaccustomed to the feeling of eyes boring through me. I held the books closer to my chest as I walked to my locker and focused wholly on turning the combination dial. As soon as I opened it, I saw a large hand slam it shut and step in front of me.

"Hey," a suave blonde boy said. I recognized him immediately. He was one of the popular fellows on the football team. He had never said a word to me prior to that day.

"What do you want?" I mumbled.

"I just want to know your name," he said with a crooked smile on the side of his face.

"Angela," I said. "Angela Lawrence."

His eyes narrowed in confusion before they popped open and his jaw dropped. He was the personification of an exclamation mark. "Angela?" He gasped. "Well… damn!"

I looked down at my shoes but couldn't suppress a tiny smile. I didn't even allow for something so remarkable in my wildest dreams. He walked down the hall to his classroom wordlessly because he was stunned, but it wouldn't be the last time he would stop by my locker.

The whole day I was floating on a cloud. I knew nothing would come of the popular boys liking me because I was so shy; the idea of saying more than a few words to a boy got my heart racing, and I didn't think I'd be able to catch my breath. Even during class I found myself staring absently at the blackboard and mindlessly doodling, my heart still thrumming away.

I continued living with Freda and the Simmonses for a couple of weeks, but there was no rest for the weary.

While on the way back from school, four boys cornered and raped me.

***

"Angela…Angela." Freda's gentle voice attempted cutting through the fog. Her face had been in the front of my field of vision, but I was only just then registering it. "The boys were caught and taken into custody."

What boys? All I knew was that my bottom was sore, always sore. Every since the broomstick incident, it bled off and on. I couldn't poo like I used to. Now it was so much worse.

"Okay," I said simply. I sat on the couch and stared ahead at the television, which was turned off. Freda squeezed my shoulder affectionately before getting up and returning to the phone.

From the rape onward, I retreated far, far within myself. All I knew was that the fantasy world I lived in was warmer and more accommodating. It was a womb where I was shrouded in comfortable darkness, oblivious to the flurry of events swirling around me. I don't remember much from that time. I walked down the street without raising my head. Going to my court dates was a tall order; facing the world head-on was too much in itself.

Though my life was darkness, as I preferred it, it was punctuated by moments of clarity. The court was a double-edged sword: the boys were found guilty, but I was required to return to Mrs. Lawrence, my legal "mother."

Before I walked back into the house, I tried gulping back my fear. I wondered previously if I were finally immune to fear; after all, what else could harm me? I had experienced everything terrible under the sun; I was sure of it. But at the sight of the brick-built, semi-detached property, my knees buckled under me. My body simply wouldn't let me move forward. I worried that if I passed over the threshold, then I would surely be sick.

Somehow, with shaky hands, I managed to open the door. Mrs. Lawrence sat on her normal perch on the couch; I immediately saw the back of her greasy brown/black hair sitting tangled at her shoulders. Once she saw me, she decided to try her hand at an underused form of torture.

"You're a slut, you deserve it." From there she bombarded me with insults and excuses, like Mrs. Simmons being unfit to have looked after me. It was "her fault" and then mine for being a slut.

I retreated back into myself immediately in blissful detachment. The last thing I remember thinking was, *God must truly hate me.*

It was back to hell—but not for good, if I had anything to do with it.

I tried running away. With no warning, I fled from the house and bolted down the street. My mind raced; I had no idea where I would go or what I would do. But unfortunately, I didn't have to worry about it long because she called the police. Somehow they found me on a playground where I sat on the swings brainstorming my next act. I cried the whole way home.

"Thank you, Officer," Mrs. Lawrence said once we returned. I stood in between two police officers—one was much younger and the other was middle-aged with a black-and-white beard. Their chests puffed out in pride at having done their duty, which sickened me.

"Please," I piped up, my voice cracking. "I can't stay here."

I just couldn't go into too much detail with the two huge burly men staring down at me; I clammed up. For a brief moment, the younger officer looked at me sorrowfully. He looked like he believed me and was trying to absorb my fear. He rolled his lips together and seemed to communicate, *I believe you.*

Mrs. Lawrence put her hand out in warning and flashed a huge smile. "I'm sorry, Officers. She's a very disobedient child and always had been, always running away, misbehaving at school…a bad, bad kid."

"That's not true!" I suddenly yelled. "She's a liar! She's a lying witch!"

The older police officer snapped his head toward me and said something I would never forget: "It sounds to me like you think the grass is greener on the other side of the fence!" I felt each word as a blow to my spirit. "What is it? Do your friends have better things than you?"

I was trembling so hard I thought I would seize. Instead I burst into tears. "You just don't get it. You just don't get it."

Before I buried my hand in my face, I saw the younger police officer looking at me with sad eyes. Surely he knew something wasn't quite right. Even if he did though, it didn't make a bit of difference. He never spoke up, and Mrs. Lawrence continued to manipulate and charm the older gentleman. Literally nobody was on my side.

❧ ❧

The taste of freedom and happiness at the Simmons's house tantalized me. I stared at the bucket in my room in disgust, and I couldn't even look at the bed where the broomstick incident had occurred. A bad taste lingered in my mouth at all times. Living with the Lawrences while growing up caused me to despise everything. My only hope was the day I would escape—whether that was through getting into a good veterinary program though my good grades, which I surprisingly managed to keep, or through dying was irrelevant to me. Both would do.

But after finally being free for a time, it was more unbearable than ever before. I crawled out from within myself and was fueled by a fire I had never known. Each time I went to the Salvation Army, I was motivated by the genuinely good people around me. Yes, good people existed, and I wanted to be with them and end my captivity. No, I did not bear the mark of the devil; I was just residing with her. This was clearer to me more than ever before.

Walking home from school, I kept my hands in my pockets and looked down as usual. I only looked up when I got to Nutley Way. I had physical reactions whenever the house came into view—if I weren't sick, I worried I would snap at any second. The two windows on either side of the exterior of the house looked like two dark, empty eyes concealing the evil within. The door below and in between the windows was the mouth, which looked a mouth agape with shock.

"No," I told myself flatly. "I'm not going in. I won't do it."

I was on the opposite end of the street and just plopped down on the stony wall lining the neighbor's house. From there I stared at the house, unable to find solace and unable to enter. So I just sat there, the overcast sky overhead, hopefully signifying imminent rain. The prospect relaxed me, and I knew somehow I'd find a solution.

After many minutes passed, I saw David exit the front door. He always returned home from school earlier than I did and must have wondered why I wasn't home yet. After looking both ways, he jogged across the road and stood in front of me. "You have to come inside," he said. "Mum knows you're here."

I stared at him for a moment before shaking my head. "No, David. I can't...I won't."

"Why not?" he asked. He glanced back at the house nervously.

"I just can't." I really couldn't scrounge up another explanation. I physically could not go back in. "Why don't you stay out here with me?"

David sighed. "If I do, she will beat me."

If for whatever reason I went back in, I would be beaten too. But it didn't matter to me. "Go ahead and go back inside, David," I said. "I'll be fine."

We stood there for a while in silence before David said, "I'm going to play football for a while and hope it doesn't rain, but I'm afraid of leaving you." Social services had started a league for teenage kids in foster care, which David loved. Thankfully Mrs. Lawrence couldn't deny him that recreation because social services were in charge of it. The last thing she wanted to do was arouse suspicion from them.

"Go," I said. "I'll be here. She can't make me go inside."

David looked at me anxiously before he said, "Okay, but I'll just be a few minutes away. Come over there if you need anything." He paused again before a spark of life flashed on his face. "Actually, I have an idea. Be right back."

David ran back inside as I continued waiting on the wall. I worried Mrs. Lawrence would detain him, but I reasoned that more than likely she would send him back out to drag me back in. As it turned out, I was right. David jogged back across the street with his left hand in a fist.

"Here," he said breathlessly. "I got this." He dropped a scrap of paper in my hand.

Curious, I accepted and unrolled it. There, in three letters, was written the name of my lifeline: *Nan*. The nine-digit number was scrawled underneath in curvy black script. David smiled at me before walking away to his practice.

Sitting cross-legged, I thought about our relationship up to that point. For every birthday, our Nan brought us birthday gifts but never set foot in the house. As I was usually in my room, I stared out the window and always saw a silver Volvo pull up. An elderly fellow always came out, our step-grandfather, Noel. The most that we were allowed was to say hello at the door, so David and I didn't really know our Nan or Noel well at all. I had no clue how David received her phone number—perhaps she suspected something terrible was going on as well.

Blood never turns to water, right? I thought. I clutched the scrap of paper near me and looked at the house across the street. Willing to take any risk necessary, I fixated on the telephone booth down the street. I found myself gravitating toward it as if being pulled on a string. Then I punched the number into the phone. It was time.

"Hello?" Nan had thankfully answered the phone.

Hearing her voice terrified and fortified me at once. "I-it's Angela," I said. "Your granddaughter."

"Angela?" I heard the surprise in her voice. It sounded like she gasped, became excited, then worried about the reason for the call in a span of three seconds. "How are you doing?"

"Not good. Nan, I can't go back into that house. I simply can't." Suddenly I found myself pouring myself out to her, not leaving out a single detail—aside from the broomstick. It was still too real to speak of. I talked about our fifth birthday, the boiling pot of water, eating my own feces, the rabbits—everything. The only interruptions were Nan's gasps and occasional tears. There was no doubt in my mind that she was appalled to the point of irrational anger at what she was hearing. By the time I finished, we were both sobbing.

"Nan, if I have to go back in there and live another day with her, I will kill myself." And I didn't just say it for dramatic effect. I was hell-bent on an escape one way or another; I was at wit's end.

"Angela, I will grab my keys right now and drive over."

My eyes welled with tears again. "Thank you."

Nan came from Boscombe, which was about a thirty-minute drive away. About twenty minutes later, however, I heard police sirens on the air. I stood up from the wall and saw flashing blue lights rippling at the end of the road, getting larger as they came closer. Nan must have called the cops!

I dove behind the wall and hoped Mrs. Lawrence couldn't see the cops or me just yet. All the while I kept my eyes out for the silver Volvo.

At each car I heard rolling up, I felt my heart drumming so hard I thought I would be sick. Right when I couldn't take it anymore though, I saw the silver Volvo. Nan stopped a couple houses before Mrs. Lawrence's, so I quickly jumped over the wall and bounded down the street. Noel was driving, and Nan was sitting in the passenger side; she motioned me to get in the backseat immediately.

"Where's David?" she asked. She was all business.

"He's at the park just a few blocks away." I said I'd guide them there.

Sure enough, we found David playing football with his friends. Once he saw my head poking out of the window, he seemed to forget what was going on and ran over to us. We whisked him up before we stopped by Mrs. Lawrence's—for hopefully the last time.

David and I opened the door, which was unlocked. There we stood in the entrance hallway with a flood of police, every member of the family, and of course Nan and Noel.

Mrs. Lawrence was livid and didn't hide it. "You f——ing b——!" she screamed. "You are a liar, a lying b——!" As I sat there calmly, she continued to call me every name under the sun. The more she did it, the less I cared: she only proved to the police what an unfit mother she really was.

But toward the end, she got especially nasty. That's when I felt a small voice rooting me on. I truly believe in that moment that God was endowing me with the strength necessary to finish my dealings with her once and for all.

"See this?" I said, literally lifting up my shirt. "*This* is what you've done. You can't call me a liar."

Everyone—the police, Nan, and Noel—saw the stormy purple-and-black bruise sprawled across my ribs. There was no mistaking it: it didn't come from a fall.

"If you want me to, I can show you the cigarette burns. I really will."

I felt Nan's protective hands on my shoulders. I turned around and saw her angry face, hard as stone, as she glared at Mrs. Lawrence. "Come on, Angie. We're leaving here."

The last I saw of Mrs. Lawrence, the police were all faced toward her, obscuring her face from my view. I don't know what happened to her after that, nor did I care. I looked straight ahead at our exit in the Volvo, never having to look at that dreadful house of horrors again.

By then it was dark and started drizzling. I smiled, knowing Mrs. Lawrence could have another reason to be depressed that night. Nan and Noel escorted David and me to their car, and we drove away, leaving the Lawrences behind.

We left and went to our Nan's. David and I had never been there, so we had no idea what to expect. When we parked in front of her house however, we wondered if we were dreaming. She had the most beautiful house I had ever seen.

"Come along then. Let's go inside," she said, waking me from my reverie. David's eyes bugged out of his face as we walked inside. It was luxury, pure luxury. Nan had money, and that was no mistake. The first thing I noticed was the smell. I closed my eyes, deeply inhaled, and smiled. There was a strange feeling within me that I had never known before; all I knew was that it felt nice.

Nan helped me figure out the word I was looking for. "Welcome home," she said, her face crinkling into a warm smile.

That night, David and I were too incandescently happy to even speak. We were comfortable but so uncomfortable at the same time. Nothing good in our lives had ever lasted before. That's when I realized I was nervous—afraid that this house and our Nan would disappear forever and we would wake back up in the Lawrences' household.

As I reflected on my conflicting feelings on the couch, Noel took a seat on the neighboring recliner, and Nan stood up beside him. They had been whispering quietly together all evening, Nan sometimes wiping a tear from her eyes. Now they were staring at us.

"Kids," she asked, "Noel and I have been talking. Would you want to live with us for now on?"

"What?" David asked immediately. His eyes continued to bulge out incredulously as they had all night. I was positive I looked the same.

"Well, yes…yes! Of course!" I blurted out. All I could think about was how much I didn't want this to be a dream. I said a silent prayer to God right then, *Please let this be real.*

"David?" Nan asked, looking earnestly looking into his face.

"Yes," he said. He turned to look at me and gave the smallest of smiles. I took ahold of his hand and whispered, "I can't believe it." He squeezed back.

Immediately, we were given nice clothes, flattering haircuts, and contact lenses for keeps. (I happily tossed my national house glasses in the trash, which I had wanted to do since I stayed at the Simmons's house.) I went into school with my full wardrobe, and no one recognized me; I fooled my classmates and took great joy in doing so.

As one could predict, our bullying was nonexistent after our move. Still, I thought about the time Mrs. Lawrence cut my white-blonde hair when I had put it into pigtails. She had always kept me by her feet while she sat at the couch, which was easier to kick and stomp on me. While I was absentmindedly watching television, I felt shears close just above my elastic band on my right ponytail. My jaw dropped in horror when I saw my white-gold hair fall in a heap beside my shoulder. After that I could only remember Mrs. Lawrence's crackly laughter; she laughed so hard she lost air and started coughing.

She prohibited me from getting a haircut or even accessing scissors to cut the other side of my hair off. The kids were merciless when I went back to school.

When I brushed my hair at my Nan's, I thought about that scenario and sighed. Though my reflection was much more favorable, I always knew that the poor girl with lopsided hair would remain a part of me. It was just too difficult to forget.

But life had its little pleasures too.

On Christmas that year, Nan nudged us awake. She was bursting at the seams with excitement to show us our gifts, and her eyes twinkled playfully. David and I happily obliged and put on our new pajamas. The smell of sausage was on the air and lured us downstairs. Our feet pattered down the cold wooden steps to the den, where a roaring fire burned beside the tree. There, right beside it, were two gleaming mountain bikes.

David and I didn't even know how to react because it was so foreign to us. Immediately my mind went to Rebecca and Amanda jumping on it and threatening to run us over. I tried to shake the mental image away.

"It's yours," Nan said. "Feel free to go try it out in the front. I'll be cooking breakfast."

She had to encourage us again to go outside and use our gifts, but once we were out, I felt like a bird. I was finally liberated to do as I pleased. The best part of it all, however, was seeing David's gleeful grin as he rolled out of the driveway. Within five minutes, our cheeks were pink and flushed from the air, which chilled us to the bone, but we didn't care. Side by side, we biked down the street and let ourselves laugh. The sun was ahead, and we were set on meeting it on the horizon.

EPILOGUE

ABUSE ISN'T A highway. I can't just speed away from it and leave it behind me until it's no bigger than a speck on the horizon. I don't choose to backtrack and linger with it. It doesn't minimize; it's not an isolated incident. Instead, it inhabits me and is a part of my makeup. There's no running from who I am and the events that shaped me; these stories inhabit my mind every day. While time heals all wounds, it doesn't always heal them to completion. Sometimes the pains are just mitigated as life irrevocably continues to unfold in front of me.

Years later, David confronted Nigel about Dad walking out those few times. "Why wasn't he there for us?" he asked. "He told us he loved us."

Nigel replied, "Dad came to my workplace and said he couldn't stand what Mum was doing to Angie and you any longer. He broke down sobbing right in front of me."

I don't know much about what happened to the Lawrences, but I do know that Mr. Lawrence separated from his wife and never returned to her. He got his own place in Bournemouth and threw himself into his work and does so to this day.

When David and I were fifteen, we moved and shared an apartment together in Bournemouth. During those times, David became aggressive and unpredictable. Finally, after much pleading from me, he told me about the abuse he suffered from Nigel and from Amanda. It has caused him extreme confusion and angst.

To my horror, I suddenly remembered hearing David and Amanda together—her telling him to touch her "there" and praising him when he did it correctly.

To this day, David struggles heavily with his memories of them. He has tried taking his life on multiple occasions, but he is thankfully now at a place of peace, having made remarkable progress with his counselors.

As for me, I now live in America with my husband, Ralph, and my sweet daughter Amber. Through them, I've come to understand and relish true love. I've found immense comfort in adopting my daughter and paving a life for her that I wish I could have had. When I hear her giggle as she plays on the slide at the park or see her gobble down watermelon with juice dribbling down her chin and a smile on her face, it slowly but surely starts filling the void inside me. I pray to be blessed with another child that God chooses for Ralph and me so that our little family can continue to grow; hopefully we can provide the loving home he or she needs, the loving home I had always desired.

I've had significant setbacks though out my life in recovering from the trauma of my youth. No matter what though, I've felt the hand of Christ in my life. He blessed me with a twin, and to this day we talk to each other every day. Inevitably we will always be concerned for one another and look out for the other's well being. David is my other half, and I have no idea what I would have done without him in my life.

Christ led me to his word through the Salvation Army; he has never and will never forsake me. I truly believe he came to me in the mirror that day at the Lawrences. While I don't know why he allowed such evil to persist, I do know that I have been given a unique perspective—a sense of empathy for all children and a loving heart. However I can use my story for the greater good, I will pursue it wholeheartedly. I hope this is just the beginning.

> "For I know the plans I have for you," declares the LORD, "plans to prosper you and not to harm you, plans to give you hope and a future."
>
> —Jeremiah 29:11 (NIV)

> And we know that in all things God works for the good of those who love him, who have been called according to his purpose.
>
> —Romans 8:28 (NIV)

The End

ACKNOWLEDGMENTS

FIRST AND FOREMOST, thank you to God, through whom all things are possible.

My Ralphie, always supportive through everything, you took time to understand how this life has taken its toll on David and me. You took the time to listen to what it has done to our hearts and souls. You understand why we are sensitive. You understand why we hide from the world. You, my love, are my rock. I appreciate that you treat me like a normal human being and not like a leper as others have and do when they find out about my childhood abuse. Thank you from the bottom of my heart for not assuming that I should have "issues" due to the abuse. You are always there through tears and laughter. I look forward growing old with you.

Amber, you have brought so much sunshine to my life. Your smile keeps my heart beating. Being your mummy is the most amazing, rewarding, enjoyable thing I have ever had the privilege to do in my life. I pray that when you are grown, you can look back and say that you had a childhood full of love. I know that you are my first thought in the morning when I awake. Even when I check on you at night, before I turn off all the lights in the house to call it a night, I watch you sleeping for a few moments. You lie there so still with a face pure as an angel's. I kiss your forehead and tell you I love you more than life itself. I lie in bed and pray for God to keep you safe and healthy and thank him for blessing Ralph and me with you. I ask God to please guide me and help me to be a good mother to you. Amber, just know that you keep me breathing. Thank you for being the most precious angel. I praise God for giving you the sweetest heart.

Danita, my dearest friend and sister from another mother, the kindness you have extended to me over the years amazes me. You never judge, and you are always there for me at the drop of a hat. When I am sick, you lay in bed with me so I don't feel alone. We talk for hours on the phone with never a pause. We finish each other's sentences. You, my sister, have never caused me harm, and we know no difference between blood and water. You are there for every life event even though you have such a busy life. My darling, you have shown me what it is to have unconditional love. Thank you for never throwing me away like a piece of garbage because I am human. You and I are one of a kind, two peas in a pod, as we often say. Having you in my life is such a blessing.

Papa and Nonnie (Steve and Angie Lombardo), my heart is full of thankfullness for the unconditional love you show me. You are always there through trials and never judge me for making mistakes. The gift of belonging is something everyone deserves and you, my treasures, gave that to me. I love you both with all my heart and soul and will never forget why now I can lift my head high.

Charlie, my faithful furry baby, since I had the privilege of finding you all alone in a cage that cold and cloudy November day thirteen years ago in that dingy pet shop in Hackney, London, I discovered what it was to be covered with love and kisses. Wherever I go, you go. Wherever I sleep, you sleep. When I feel lost, you always manage to make my heart beat with glee. I never feel alone when you are around. Charlie, I was alone until you. David was so sick, and I had no one. You filled my life with joy and love. You were and still are my everything. I thank you, my buddy, for always laying at my feet and making me feel like I belong.

Endless thank yous to Louise Jenkins and Jeanette Holland from Irwin Mitchell Solicitors. You brought us justice. You went above and beyond for David and me. Thank you for taking our story to heart and fighting for us ceaselessly. Thanks to you, we have closure.

Last but certainly not least, my twin, David, I'm almost rendered speechless as I attempt to write this because so many emotions flood through me. You are my other half. You are my anchor. When I had no one else and when my only hope and expectation out of life was death, you endowed me with purpose. Some people might not understand what it is to love someone more than themselves or to value another life more than their own. For you and me, it's natural. You were and will always remain my treasure. The years have been hard, and we will still have our moments, but we can get through anything as we always have: together.